Law of Attraction

Successfully Manifest Love, Abundance, Happiness and Wealth

(Raise Your Vibrations Using Visualizations and Begin Your Spiritual Journey)

Emma Graham

Published By **Oliver Leish**

Emma Graham

All Rights Reserved

Law of Attraction: Successfully Manifest Love, Abundance, Happiness and Wealth (Raise Your Vibrations Using Visualizations and Begin Your Spiritual Journey)

ISBN 978-1-77485-588-1

No part of this guidebook shall be reproduced in any form without permission in writing from the publisher except in the case of brief quotations embodied in critical articles or reviews.

Legal & Disclaimer

The information contained in this ebook is not designed to replace or take the place of any form of medicine or professional medical advice. The information in this ebook has been provided for educational & entertainment purposes only.

The information contained in this book has been compiled from sources deemed reliable, and it is accurate to the best of the Author's knowledge; however, the Author cannot guarantee its accuracy and validity and cannot be held liable for any errors or omissions. Changes are periodically made to this book. You must consult your doctor or get professional medical advice before using any of the suggested remedies, techniques, or information in this book.

Upon using the information contained in this book, you agree to hold harmless the Author from and against any damages, costs, and expenses, including any legal fees potentially resulting from the application of any of the information provided by this guide. This disclaimer applies to any damages or injury caused by the use and application, whether directly or indirectly, of any advice or information presented, whether for breach of contract, tort, negligence, personal injury, criminal intent, or under any other cause of action.

You agree to accept all risks of using the information presented inside this book. You need to consult a professional medical practitioner in order to ensure you are both able and healthy enough to participate in this program.

Table of Contents

Chapter 1: Basics & Fundamentals 1

Chapter 2: Finding Love And Loving Yourself 5

Chapter 3: Law Of Attraction 20

Chapter 4: What We Think Is What We Are 33

Chapter 5: Law Of Attraction 39

Chapter 6: The Reality Of Our Desire 45

Chapter 7: The Body 57

Chapter 8: Unlock Your Ultimate Potential 72

Chapter 9: Let Go Of Your Thoughts 88

Chapter 10: Millionaire Strategies To Use The Law Of Attraction In Order To Reach Your Goals 95

Chapter 11: The Happiness Factor 115

Chapter 12: Myths Or Truths 120

Chapter 13: How The Law Of Attraction Works 137

Chapter 14: Belief 151

Chapter 15: Rethinking Your Mind 166

Chapter 16: The Secret To Attraction Law 170

Chapter 17: Establishing Regular Self-Hypnosis Procedures 175

Conclusion 183

Chapter 1: Basics & Fundamentals

Ancient teachers, mystics, and philosophers tried to teach us about how the Law Of Attraction works. Many great works have been published that show the power of the Law Of Attraction. Many are still unaware of the Law Of Attraction's true power, meaning and purpose. It does not matter how well you understand the law. The Law Of Attraction still works every minute of every day. Isn't this time for you to understand how to use the Universal Principle and make it work for your benefit?

At its basic level, the Law Of Attraction states, "Everything is created by thought" and that it attracts to itself people, places, circumstances, and physical objects. These things are all at your fingertips, right now!

Our creative abilities affect not only the external world, but all of it. Every aspect of our lives, including our personality and traits, is affected by our creative thinking. Are you creating and living the life you desire? Or do you feel like Job, bringing all sorts of problems upon yourself because you pay too much attention to them. Maybe you are even calling yourself a victim of the Law, refusing it to be acknowledged and used consciously.

Although it was revealed in "The Secret", this law has been kept secret for centuries. The Law Of Attraction isn't as secretive as people think. It has existed since the beginning and it is unchanging, unbending, and unbreakable. It cannot be ignored. There is ample evidence that shows mankind has known of and used the great Law since approximately 7000 BC. However, the teachings and application of universal truths got clouded by greedy dogmatists who desired to keep the masses in control.

The diligence, fortitude and grace that writers such Charles Haanel (1866-1949) displayed in their writings, Napoleon Hill (1883-1970), James Allen (1864-1912), Charles Haanel

(1866-349), and Charles Haanel (1866-349) made this law more widely known.

Wallace D. Wattles (born in 1860; died in 1911) was a forward-thinking person. Wattles writes in his masterpiece "The Science Of Getting Rich" that "There's a thinking stuff from where all things are made. In its original state it permeates through the universe, penetrates and then fills all interspaces. The thought within this substance is what produces the thing that is imaged in the thought. What a revolutionary statement that was in 1910.

Haanel created a correspondence course in 24 parts. This is now "The Master Key System", one volume that explains how to use the Law Of Attraction. Its revelations were so shocking that the Church expelled it from its ranks in 1933. This is the book Bill Gates was said to have read before he created Microsoft.

Napoleon Hill revealed Andrew Carnegie's great Secret to Success - that ideas create things — in his 1937 novel "Think & Grow Rich", though it took him 25+ years to complete.

James Allen wrote his famous 1912 book, "As One Man Thinketh". He tells people that mind is the master weaver, of the inner and outer clothing of character as well as of circumstances.

Although these teachings have existed for thousands of year and have been freely and easily available to almost every person for the past century, the majority of people never take the time and learn about the most powerful law in the Universe.

It's your responsibility to study the laws of life and dig deeper into the universe. You will experience a profound understanding of the Law Of Attraction that you can use to your advantage. Your life will change in amazing, unexpected, and endless ways.

Chapter 2: Finding Love And Loving Yourself

Make Your Life Board

This chapter is the first of 21 days to a better way of living.

It is important to get to know yourself first before you can change your life.

It is essential to have a clear understanding about yourself before you can find your purpose and your way in life.

Grab some colorful pens and large sheets of paper or illustration.

This board will become your personal journal and guide you in your quest to discover yourself.

This is your chance to create your own happiness project.

Create two (2) large columns on your Life Board.

Mark the first column with the label GOOD and in this column list down your present traits/characteristics.

In the second column, label BEST with the word BEST. Below this column, write down what you want to change about your life, your dreams, goals, and your deepest hopes and aspirations.

It is possible to look in the mirror to see all of your features. Next, examine the intangibles.

Ask yourself candid and open questions about all aspects of yourself.

Start with the most obvious.

Gradually work your path to intangible traits like being "intuitive" or always eager to learn.

Ask yourself: "Am I calm, collected, forgiving?" Or "Am I quick with anger and judgmental of others?"

Ask your spiritual self questions about whether you believe in God, and if so, how. You don't need to adhere to any particular religion. It is up to you to decide if you believe that there is an Higher Being responsible.

After you have become more aware of yourself, you can accept these traits as who and what you are.

More concretely, you can assess the physical, psychological, and spiritual aspects of your self to get a candid, open-minded, honest-to-goodness look at yourself.

You've now examined yourself in the mirror. Next, you need to examine how you see yourself.

Do you accept yourself completely?

Do you love and accept yourself, despite all your imperfections and flaws?

Day One is intended to give you a clear idea of yourself as well your desires and hopes.

Given all these traits, whether they are good or not, create a checklist to list all you want to change in your 21-day journey toward a better you.

Start with the small things.

Keep a list of everything that you wish to do on your Life Board.

You can write as much as you like.

It can be creative and colorful. You may also draw it if desired.

You must make sure what you write reflects your goals for the long-term, short-term and medium-term.

There are no impossible goals.

Everything is possible.

This magic list will contain everything you need to know about your future and present plans.

It may be 21 days of journey to a happier life. However, the 22nd day and the remainder of the other days make up the rest.

You can think of the next 21 day as the first step to becoming a better and more vibrant version you.

Then, days 22 through the rest of you life will turn into one fantastic journey where you steadily attain all that you set your mind to.

Making a change in your life for the better can be a painful and long process.

You have taken the first critical step to reclaim your life and move forward with your life by creating your Life Board.

Your Life Board now has images or visualisations. This is a great way for you to see yourself reaching your goals and achieving success.

This Life Board will become your guideline for the next 21 day and beyond.

Detoxify and declutter your mind

Day one was about creating your Life Board. This allowed you to reflect on your life and make projections onto your long-term and short term goals.

Today, we are going to take a closer glance at our inner selves and outer selves.

Ask yourself the following questions.

* Do You feel bloated and bloated.

* Do you sweat profusely?

* Are you suffering from debilitating headaches or severe migraines?

* Are your eyes constantly tired?

* Do your mood swings often?

* Do your thoughts wander and you are unable to focus?

* Do you suffer from poor digestion and allergic reactions

If you experience any one of these symptoms, then you might be suffering from toxic overdose.

However, don't be discouraged! Today we will help you feel healthier and more rejuvenated.

The best way to detoxify your body is by eating three well-chosen meals per day, and allowing your body to digest them for at least five to six hours in between.

You can allow your body and organs to have the time they need to process the food in the five-hour interval between meals.

Fresh fruits, vegetables, and other vegetables are great for detoxifying the body.

Avoid carbonated or fizzy beverages, alcoholic drinks and coffee. You can enjoy herbal or organic green teas.

At least ten (10) glasses of water are recommended daily. While it might seem like a lot of water and may cause you to visit the bathroom often, your body will eventually adjust.

If you find plain water boring, add lemon, lime honey, ginger and other health benefits to it.

It is important to plan your meals in advance. You will need three portions (three portions) of vegetables, three pieces of fruit, three salads, two portions of nuts, and one portion brown rice.

If you can, eat your last meal not later than 7:00pm.

This gives your body enough time to absorb the food before you go bed.

After cleansing your body, you can take a deep breathing and gather your thoughts.

You can start today to practice deep breathing for at least five minute each day.

It is a sad fact, but it is true that breathing becomes more shallow and irregular when we feel anxious or tense.

Learn to breathe in a deep and correct manner. It will cleanse the body from toxins and teach you how to relax.

More importantly, if we practice deep breathing correctly and consistently, we begin to feel calmer and less stressed.

Like the waves in the ocean, our chaotic lives are slowly becoming calmer and more peaceful.

Keep these things in mind as you go.

Cleanse your body and mind with the right foods and quality deep breathing.

These two steps will make an enormous difference on your 21-day journey toward a better, more fulfilling life and a fresh start!

There will be moments during the 21 day journey when you want to just eat as much as possible.

Instead of letting it all go and giving up on it, extinguish any negative thoughts and take five minutes of deep quality breath.

These negative thoughts, and defeatist thinking, are to be expected.

Don't think about them.

They are thoughts that you can just banish.

Now, you can relax, get a restful night's sleep, then get ready for Day 3.

The Body is Your Workplace

Your 21-day journey to a better you will have some setbacks the first few times.

As your body adapts to the new diet you may experience constipation, loose bowel movement or diarrhea.

Do not be worried

This is normal and a sign of your body cleansing out all toxins.

Start exercising while you continue with your detoxifying routine from now to the end.

Exercise is an excellent way to improve your metabolism rate and get your body going.

Be sure to consult your doctor before you start any exercise program.

Walking, swimming and biking are some of the safest exercises.

Avoid exercising if your body hasn't had a rest for some time.

Walking gently and easily stimulates the heart muscle, lungs, heart, and brain. Begin slowly by starting with 10-15 minutes each day. Gradually increase the time to 30. Walking fast enough will cause a slight sweat.

Swimming is good for all major muscle groups.

Cycling is a great form of exercise that can help build endurance and tone the legs.

A bike that isn't your own can offer the same benefits as an exercise bike.

You can also bounce a trampoline up to 15 minutes per day.

Do not rush to complete any exercise.

Do not force yourself to the limit.

Find an exercise that allows you to relax and clears your mind.

Even housework counts towards exercise. An hour of vigorous housework can be as effective as a visit to the gym. The act of cleaning floors can burn as much as 400 calories an hour.

Exercise is good not only for your body, but also for the mind and spirit.

It should also have fun and be interesting.

If you are not good at dancing, learn to dance.

There is no such thing a dancer who doesn't know how to move.

You may just be looking for the right partner.

Don't be afraid to get up and dance, no matter what the music is. It will improve your health.

Your body will love it.

You can start today and go every day after that to make time for your daily walk or jog in the local area.

Scientists have shown that exercise, including walking, can increase the release of endorphins.

It's clear that exercise makes you feel happier inside and out.

You will be happier with your body and have the confidence to wear the stylish business suits or sexy dresses you have always dreamed of but were unable to fit into.

You can now slim down by working out and losing weight!

Laughter, the best medicine

For the first 3 days, you will be able to visualize our goals, cleanse ourselves of our mind, and tone our muscles to become a fitter.

Let's reexamine today the importance laughter has in our lives.

You're familiar with the lyrics of that song: "Don't worry. Just be happy."

Do you remember the last time that you went on a wild and hilarious laughter trip?

People find that laughing can help them cope with everyday stress.

Scientific research has shown that people who use humour in dealing with stressful experiences are less tired, more angry, and less depressed.

Laughter can help relax facial muscles as well as deepen your breathing. Laughter increases blood flow, improves blood pressure, and exercises the internal muscles.

Laughter, much like exercise and other forms of laughter, can release endorphins. These endorphins are natural painkillers for the body.

So what are your waiting for?

Read a book or story that is funny. Enjoy a funny movie or your favourite sitcom.

A good chuckle can make life much more pleasant.

Chapter 3: Law Of Attraction

How should it be used?

This will give you an overview of the LoA and the reasons so many people have adopted this. You should have a greater understanding of the LoA before diving into the book.

LoA not only makes a statement regarding attraction, but it also suggests how to look at situations in your life. In particular, it encourages us not to see a lack of abundance but instead to see the possibility of having plenty. The following are examples to illustrate.

You can decide if you are in an abundance or scarcity mindset.

1. You are contemplating whether you will help a business associate with a project. It is a very likely project and you feel you can contribute to its success. Your decision to cancel your new project comes down to this: You are not willing to lose one client because

a small segment of your customer base overlaps.

2. The fact that you have not done this before makes it difficult for you to make a decision about whether you should start an affiliate programme to promote your new product. Instead of seeking assistance, you have decided that the program will probably fail.

3. You just started a business. You would like to rent an office so you can send your staff. It is obvious that this is a big risk. However, instead of letting it get you down, you choose to ignore it and continue to work hard, regardless how difficult it may seem at first.

4. You are debating whether or not to do something for your spouse (husband). You are aware that you could make your wife's life easier by pleasing her husband, but ultimately you choose not to. Instead, it is decided to refuse the offer.

These examples show you the difference between an abundance mentality (or a lack thereof) and a short-sighted mentality (or both). Can you see the LoA giving you direction about how to think, behave and generate kindness and cooperation from others?

You will be able see that you don't need to worry so much about being taken advantage off and live your life as if you were doing nothing but extracting every penny and favor you could from others.

These are crucial points to remember about the LoA if it is your intention to use it properly and reap all the rewards.

How do we know it works

Many people advise that you shouldn't worry about whether the LoA is successful. You shouldn't worry about whether positive thinking or having an abundance mentality produces better results.

But i do not agree. As with everything you do in your life, work, and personal relationships, you need to determine if what you have done is actually producing results. This is vital so you can improve and refine your approach as well as determine if it really works.

This is true regardless of what anyone tries to tell you.

You might initially view this as a contradiction. It is possible to believe that it can be positive.

Maintaining some degree of skepticism. It is actually possible.

How can it be done? You can start by setting up a trial. Consider allowing yourself three months. Then, commit to following the Law of Attraction.

You should not let anything hinder you from achieving the goals that you set for yourself during the trial. Keep your mind positive and fixate on your goals.

You can also think in "abundance" while you are on trial.

Remember to behave as if you already have your goals. What would you do if you were as smart, wealthy, pleasant, well-informed, and attractive as you wish to be? It would be a shame, it is not. It is also not the best way to live if you are trying to achieve your objectives.

Try it for three months and give it everything you have. Then, see what happens. I promise you that living in abundance, positive thinking, constructive giving, and not expecting anything in return will change your life, your company, and your relationships.

Why cynicism seems inappropriate

Many people make the error of thinking that skepticism, especially when it is related to the LoA. However, there is nothing wrong in skepticism. There is nothing wrong about thinking things through before signing a contract. There is nothing wrong with asking whether the berries that were picked from the forest are edible or toxic.

Skepticism, which can improve our performance and preserve our lives, is essential.

Cynicism is an entirely different animal. Cynicism is the belief that there is no hope for us and that we cannot be successful. We create something totally contrary to the LoA.

We often forget that our goal is to attract good things into our lives through visualizations and actions, and instead we concentrate on the things that are not working.

If you are serious in the LoA practice to achieve your goals and strengthen your relationships as well as your work and business success, then cynicism needs to be replaced. You have to replace it, with a consistent and constant motivation to overcome difficulties.

Why are visualization and focus so important

The law of attraction states, "If you concentrate on the positive things in your life, then positive things will come to your life." LoA supporters stress that we should set aside some time during the day for things we wish to see in our lives.

If you are a new practitioner of LoA, it is important to set aside time every day for this. Your objectives should be clearly defined and you should spend several hours setting them out. Don't focus on obtaining a certain sum of money, but instead think about how you could use it to make your life better, buy the house you want, and so forth.).

After you've defined your goals, devote at least half an hr each day to focusing on them. You can then visualize it happening. Although it might sound extreme at first, many professionals, successful athletes, and entrepreneurs use this method on a daily basis.

You'll soon understand why it is so useful once you have done it a few times. It helps you concentrate your attention on what is important: achieving your goals.

It helps to carefully walk through your goals, one step at a time, using visualization. This is important as it will help create a detailed plan to overcome any obstacles and achieve your goals, no matter how hard they might seem.

Instruct your children to visualize and focus in a positive environment

Focus and visualization are essential parts of the LoA application. If you can concentrate on your goals, can visualize them becoming a reality, and are willing to accept the results, then the LoA will work for you. This will allow you to reap the personal and material benefits.

It is important that you think about how to increase your focus, and strengthen your visualization abilities. These techniques can be used to improve your ability to focus, calm nerves, and your thinking.

1. Consider lighting an aromatherapy candle, or burning incense. Make sure you choose a scent which will help you focus and give you

energy. Do not use a smell that is too strong or dull. To achieve this goal, you can use flavors such as mint, grapefruit or vanilla. After the aroma has settled in the room, focus on your goals and close your eyes. Visualize it, then accept it.

2. Get a massage. Massages can help relax and calm your muscles. This will make it easier for you to keep your eyes on one thing, which is the process to achieve your goal.

3. A warm bath is a good idea. This will help you relax and concentrate. Concentrate your thoughts on one goal and how to reach it.

4. Meditation is a practice. Meditation is one technique that helps you to focus on one thought. The LoA will be more effective if you learn to meditate.

Focus and visualization are important aspects of the LoA. Focusing and visualizing well are two important aspects of the LoA.

How to avoid having negative thoughts

Cynicism can cause us to lose the LoA, as I already mentioned. Because it can discourage you from working harder because it will convince us that nothing is possible. You'll lose your ability to focus on a goal and follow-through.

It is therefore important to avoid negative thoughts and cynical views if you truly wish to apply the law.

Instead, try to focus on positive ideas that can reinforce our culture.

Vision of the Future

How can we accomplish this? There are many possible ways. These are just a few of the many options.

1. Learn how to avoid thinking evil thoughts

If you are re-inforcing negative thoughts with more, then you must find a way of breaking free from that destructive cycle. When this happens, psychologists recommend that you use Cognitive Behavioral Therapy or (CBT).

One popular CBT technique is to use an elastic band around the wrist. If you are having negative thoughts, snap the elastic. This will give you an immediate, tangible feedback and can help you stop thinking negative thoughts.

Alternate methods include interrupting what you are currently doing to do something else. It could happen that you are looking at a lot of papers and feel depressed.

Instead of sitting still and staring at paperwork, get up and walk around. Get a cup and a chat with someone in the cubicle nearby. This can help stop the negative cycle from getting started.

2. Avoid any place(s) that promote negative thoughts

Bad thoughts can easily occur in your daily experiences. Maybe you were affected by an unanticipated event in your life that caused you failure. Or, perhaps something terrible happened to you or your family. Evil thoughts will return every time that you visit that location.

It's time for you to stop visiting those places in your life. Yes, one place can make a person sad. However, there is little you can do to get rid of that sadness. Consider a different route.

Avoid all places that may lead to you becoming more negative.

3. Keep your relationships healthy and wise.

If you have friends that constantly criticize and question you or your abilities, then it is time to meet new people. Although it is important to have someone to challenge you in your circle or group of influence to exchange constructive thoughts, it is seldom helpful to have someone to criticize you and find hundreds (unlikely!) ways that your ideas might fail.

This strategy will not accomplish anything. However, it will allow you to focus on positive thoughts. Review your current relationships from time-to-time.

Determine if the friends with whom you have made friends can help you improve your life and make you more successful or if it is dragging down your progress.

The LoA can basically be summarized in 3 easy steps. 1. Think deeply about what you are most passionate about. Second, it is important to be focused on one thing in order to attract that particular thing into your life. You must be open and willing to accept what you want, even when you initially feel afraid to achieve it.

LoA can also be described as focusing and visualization. It is important to see abundance as a possibility, rather than scarcity. The next chapters will focus on specific ways to apply the LoA in order to improve your daily life.

Chapter 4: What We Think Is What We Are

The energy around us is the same energy as that which flows through us, and this is the first step towards true enlightenment. The law of attraction is a principle that has been influential and paving the way for greatness since ancient times.

The notion that we could create our very own worlds through thinking seems incredible. Although we live in a time in which so much is known about myths or ancient beliefs, it is not difficult to think like that. We also live in a period of great discovery. Science opens up new possibilities every day.

The mind that isn't closed will always be closed.

Many new ideas and concepts have been unravelled by quantum physics's breakthroughs and new research. We don't necessarily need to know the world to be able make our own ideas come true using the law of attraction. While you don't necessarily need to be an expert in the sciences to understand the law, it can be interesting to see what science is uncovering that is related to the basic laws.

This was mind blowing when it was revealed that an electron could theoretically exist in two distinct places at the exact same time. This meant that each thing could be located in more than one place simultaneously.

In theory, how we view the world may be different from what others see. Our minds have a greater impact on the world than we thought. NLP refers this to the map, where perception plays a significant role. The law of attraction also requires us to think about perception so we can manifest the right stuff.

Our brains are wired in a way to see patterns. It is part of our survival instinct. For survival, our brains had to recognize patterns around us at one point. This is how we are able to quickly identify things that we recognize by simply looking at an abstract pattern. faces. Our brains are driven to make sense from all the information and so create patterns out almost nothing. Can we really rely on our brains for the truth?

Many experiments show that it is possible to trick our brains in this manner. What does this prove? It shows that what we perceive is often not what we actually see.

We can use the same basic idea to show that what we think we want is not always actually what we want.

People make this common error when using the law. They believe that what they think will manifest as if by magic. It is important to remember that the power does not rest in the thoughts.

What does this statement tell us?

I need more funds

It is a simple message telling you that the person has no money. The likelihood of them attracting more is increased if they have less money. This means that less money is more of what you want. Can you see how this is a problem?

Also, it is crucial to be mindful of what we believe. Thinking of abundance as something already in your life would be far better. It sends the message that it is already there. You will attract more of that same. Take the "money always goes back to money" statement as an example.

Optimism

It is essential to emphasize that this stage does not allow anyone to blame the law or attract for their unhappiness. It is not an excuse for poor decision making or a 'get-out' clause.

To fully grasp the laws, it is important that you also have an optimistic mindset. It doesn't matter if you learn to harness the power to attract with conscious thought or design. It's happening in your real life.

A person who is naturally attuned to the laws of attraction is known as an optimist. They might not be consciously manifesting what it is they want, but they attract fair amounts of abundance by using their natural optimism and focusing on the right thoughts.

This isn't imagination.

For proof that the law of attraction works, just look at your optimist friend. They'll be more relaxed and in good health than those around them. They will have brighter perspectives on the world and expect good things in the end. Optimists just have more positive energy. They are less likely be tempted to give up, and they tend to be more optimistic. They can also expect things to go their way, which often leads to them being successful in business. Optimists know how to tap into all the possibilities of the universe.

If you have a friend who thinks in this manner, you will soon understand why. The same thing is occurring with opposite outcomes to the pessimistic person. The likelihood of someone who views the world with a doom & gloom outlook is that they will live a life in which things don't seem to be going their way. There are many types of this. Someone who is kind but pessimistic might attract kindness back from people trying to help. But, the most important signal they are sending is one that lacks, and so they end up with what they want.

This is the way people live their lives. There's no thought of how to change it. Understanding how different thought patterns can make a difference in your life will help you understand the law of attraction.

This is just the beginning of many people's journey.

Chapter 5: Law Of Attraction

This universal law states, "Like attracts Like" and is fundamentally focused on the idea of positive and negative attracting each other. All of this is to say that we, as human beings, are in total control of the events in our lives. This is due to the fact we control all of our thoughts and feelings. Everything that happened to or against you was attracted to it. According to the law, success can be achieved by asking, believing, and receiving.

Your thoughts are what will decide how successful you are in life. Positive thinking and believing in something increases your chances of reaching it. Your thoughts are what create and bring about whatever you think. The universe is always interested in what signals we send. It will deliver exactly the results we desire.

Believe me, you will succeed in life if your self-deprecating thoughts about yourself or the things you have to do will continue. Be positive and give yourself credit. You will feel more inspired to do better in the future. This is what your life should be about. Trusting your abilities and sacrificing anything that you can, even negative thoughts.

Did you ever go into an exam with a preconceived notion that you didn't know much about that course or that you would have little chance of passing? Your mind becomes completely locked up and you'll be unable answer even the simplest questions. Part of you knows you lack the knowledge and skills to answer these questions. It's a great idea to get up in the morning and just tell your self everything will work out. This will increase your self-esteem and confidence which will allow you to accomplish the largest part of the interview. While some things might seem difficult at first glance, you should give it another chance before you make any judgments.

Positive thinking is the best way for you to live your life. It not only helps you get the things you desire, but it also makes you a better person by improving your well-being.

Your life will be more fulfilling if you have a positive outlook. You will attract positive people to your life. The best thing for us is to appreciate and embrace what's good. Only then can we live happily.

No matter how conscious or unconscious we are, we are always responsible for the positive and bad influences that are brought into our lives. Understanding the law o f attraction is a crucial step that will allow us to achieve all the good things in our lives. The outcome of what you do will depend on where your attention is placed. Although we may not be aware of it, we are often the ones who make our lives feel meaningless. The law that attracts you is something you should understand. If you want your life to be more positive, then you must start feeding your mind positivity.

What happened in your past, or how dire your present situation may be, should not determine your future. It doesn't matter if you believe it, but you have the potential to make a great living. You have control over your life, and you can shape it as you wish. While there will be times when things do not go your way, it is possible to improve them instead of assuming that this is the only way you are destined to be. The power to change and shape the course of our lives is ours. Research shows that we all are susceptible to the law if attraction, regardless our age, nationality, beliefs or religion. This law is exactly what makes use the power of the mind and transforms our thoughts into realities.

There is no reason to stay silent about the law. Although the law has been a long-standing mystery, it is becoming increasingly well-known for its significant impact on everyday life. To stick to the law, you can use affirmations or vision boards. One thing you need to know is that luck doesn't exist. The more you work hard, the more luck you will have. The law o' attraction is supposed to help you believe and be open to all possibilities.

THE LAW OF CAUSES AND EFFECT

The universal law of cause-and-effect is another universal law. It states that nothing happens by chance in life and that each action must result in an equal and opposite reaction. It is believed that the cause of a person's actions, words and thoughts is their thought. This causes them to create a wave effect, which then in turn creates an effect. This is why it is said that good actions, good emotions and good thoughts are vital for a better world. This law states that every cause is affected by every effect. Every effect then becomes the cause.

All humans need to realize that their actions can have an effect on how the world turns out. This will help them make every effort to improve the lives of everyone. You cannot sit still and expect to be financially independent. All things in life happen for a reason. Conscious or unconscious choices have corresponding results.

I believe that now you understand this law you are able to know what is necessary to attract the best. It basically teaches us that hardwork is crucial to being successful. This is especially true if your goal to build a lasting relationship with your spouse. Perhaps you've heard about karma. This teaches us that everyone reaps what he or she puts in, and it's exactly the same thing.

This should make your eyes see the reality of life. Success is possible if you are determined to succeed. You now have a clear understanding of what the word means. Therefore, it is important to create and implement action plans that will help you achieve your goals. Take these universal laws as your guide and you will be able to make a better living.

Chapter 6: The Reality Of Our Desire

Do you ever notice how some people can accomplish the right things in the right context, with the right people at the correct time and with the right circumstances. It seems like everything is in their favor and they can pull it off again. They make it look easy.

Imagine if I told them that they had a simple secret. It is possible that some of them might not put it this way but they all share one secret.

They wanted the results that they got. I'm sure that you're probably rolling in your eyes. You may be laughing so loud that you're actually stuttering. Isn't everyone looking for the best things in life? Does everyone want the best life?

I get where you are coming. Be aware that although successful people desire great results, they are not the same as everyone else.

What is the difference between successful and unsuccessful people?

Successful people desire certain results just like everybody else.

It is not that people wish or hope for everything they desire. People think that somehow, someway, things will come together. Maybe they will even get the results they desire.

Succession depends on what your background is and how much money you have. But they do it differently. They let their passion drive them unlike others.

From feelings to Goals

Succession is more than just being able to relax and experience the warm, fuzzy feeling most people get when they live in an alternate reality. They feel an intense rush of emotions and don't let that stop.

Instead, they let themselves be so hyped up about a desired result that they break down the information into who, what, where and when. They know the reasons. They are able to feel the reasons they want. They're not as concerned about the details. They start at end.

Do you wish to be rich? How rich do you want to be? How much wealth do you need to consider yourself rich?

Where would you want to live? Can you describe the house Can you describe your backyard? What's your backyard like? What kinda car would you drive?

Who are your neighbors like? What kind of activities would you enjoy with your neighbors? Where would it be best to vacation?

Succession requires that you define your desired outcome. Then they can piece together the goals. In this way, they move beyond the feeling of wishing and hope, which can lead them to feel very strong emotions. They are able to describe and measure their goals, and then put them into a timeline.

This is a significant leap for many people. Because we're so obsessed with our dream reality, we stop at the intense emotion state. Many times, we do not want to change reality. In other cases, we just want emotional rewards.

Maybe your relationship doesn't seem as fulfilling or rewarding. So you imagine your partner as Prince Charming. Or maybe you meet the perfect princess. And you place emphasis on the emotion of that person.

Problem is, if you're focusing on your hopes and desires, you're actually triggering positive emotions. These can sometimes make it impossible to be responsible for the things happening in your world right now.

It's not surprising that many people live in unhappy relationships. The same applies to jobs, businesses and educational pathways-- you can't go wrong. Too many of our lives never reach the point where we can truly move from wish and hope to our goals.

Successful people do. They don't do this once in a while.

You can turn random thoughts into reality

I have met many successful people who are very careful with their words.

If they aren't close to their goal, they won't say "I will do something", because it is impossible to tell them. They'd rather not release any press releases or make an announcement until they are confident that they will succeed.

This is what most people say to you. You'd hear them say, "Well, I'm going make a change in my life," or "I'm gonna turn things around," or "I'm gonna lose weight," but this has to stop.

There are many versions of those statements. But the sad reality of the matter is that the majority of people don't transform their thoughts into realities. This, however, is the norm for successful people. How?

They tap into the power of desires.

Through the emotional force, you can create the reality that you desire.

Please think back to the previous description.

Feeling hopeful and optimistic can cause a rush in your emotions. You get the feeling that you can make things happen, and that no matter how grim your situation, there is hope. This is what wishing, hoping and praying does.

These emotions are what makes successful people shine. You want something different. To create this alternative reality, it is necessary to change your behavior now.

To bring about that change, you must first zero in on your emotions. Once you do, let the desire to make that happen drive you to set goals and then sub-goals.

This strong emotional state will enable you to alter your verbal behaviors. This is self-talk, which I mentioned in this book.

Focusing on your desired reality will help you tap into your powerful emotions and change the internal monologue you're repeating to yourself. Then you will start taking new actions.

These strong emotions may have been there before you ever started to view your desire in a different light. They did their job. A low point in the day was when you felt lost, angry or bitter. You then start to imagine a different way of living your life.

Maybe you can find a partner, who is accepting of you as you truly are. Perhaps you envision yourself in another city or country, living a completely different lifestyle.

This emotional state increases based on the things you're focusing your mental attention on. It also helps to get rid of negative feelings that you may have about your current reality.

However, this emotional state can start to break down, and you're back to your reality.

This is the most common way people deal with desires. It is a dream, a figment of our imagination.

Successful people use desire to create positive feedback loops

They feel that same strong emotion, and successful people are no different to you. The difference with them is that their actions are driven by it.

Do not get too excited about the prospect of earning more. Let your feelings give you the power to accomplish what you need.

This could involve looking at passive income sources, online earning opportunities, or using your strong emotional drive to overcome your reluctance to learn new skills or take up an instructional program.

Whatever your situation may be, let the power that is desire work with you mind and heart to help you find a better way. Once you know the path ahead, make it a point to desire to change.

By taking positive action towards your goals, you create a positive feedback system. You start to realize you are not just wishing or hoping. You're not waiting for the world around you to change.

Instead, taking an action can bring about changes in your life. Once you recognize that you are in control, you will take another action. And another. And so on. You'll eventually get there.

Your power increases each time you take a step that you might not or be afraid to take. Things do not have to be the same. You don't need to feel powerless. You can make some changes. And you can do it!

These small changes are the seeds that start to change.

The power in mustard seeds

Jesus Christ said to his disciples, "If you have only the faith of one mustard seed, you will be able to move mountains," in the Bible.

If you take small actions, you are demonstrating to yourself the power and desire of action. From fear and inertia to action, you can move beyond fear, risk aversion, and outright fear. When you see the outcomes of your actions, you will realize how much power is available to change the course of your life.

Now, you're ready to take another action. Then you take another. As their consequences grow over time, your life begins to change.

You could have been living a life of disappointment, mediocrity and frustration. Now, you realize that applying to an online course will lead to a decision not to quit and show up for the work. If you make the decision to take an online course, you will be able to gain greater knowledge and have more opportunities to learn. This allows you to use the knowledge.

Before you know you know it, your certificate is issued and you are ready to apply for online freelance jobs using the skills you just learned. Maybe it's content marketing, SEO, and scripting languages like Python or C++.

There are many ways to move forward, but the first step is the most important. It is possible for a small step to seem insignificant like a mustard-seed. However, if you trust enough in your desired reality, you can take larger and more significant steps.

Start small. Don't be afraid. You already have it in yourself.

It's not just a theory. You start to feel more confident. This isn't just an assumption about what could happen. It's something you've witnessed happen. You had the courage and resources to register for a course. You now move on to the next step.

In the world that is relationships, you had the courage and the ability to confront your partner about problems in your relationship. Now it's time to move on.

At work, your boss encouraged you to ask for a raise. It is now that you are ready to move on.

You feel that certain areas of your daily life should be taken for granted. They're not. You can make a shift. It's as easy as a person to awaken the power within them to make a change. That strong emotion will allow you to take control of your actions and decisions.

Chapter 7: The Body

The body is an excellent way to practice self love. It's the easiest and most effective way to practice self-love. It doesn't require much concentration on the inner you. You can move your whole body and completely forget your thoughts. You might need to be silent for certain types of exercise. Yoga is a practice that allows your thoughts to wander. Running and swimming are great ways to relieve stress, improve your flexibility, and help you move your joints. It may prove difficult for others depending on their abilities. I'm here to tell that you can move your body in any way you choose. I believe that there is a way to allow everyone to move their bodies in a healthy and individual way.

You can exercise your body to learn self-love. You don't need to be an athlete. However, studies have shown that exercise is something your body craves.

You may hate cardio. It's fine. Consider doing a light version of yoga. While you may dislike stretching, there are other options. For example, try boxing. It will help you in your journey to self-love by finding the best movement for you and/or your body. Self-love can be a journey, especially in relation to your body. One month you may choose to run, the next time you will be lifting weights. You can let your body decide what you want. Move your body and get out of your comfort zones. Water aerobics may be the perfect hobby for you.

You may find that moving your whole body can help you align mind and heart. Nature is an example of this. It is possible to be in nature and get away from the daily hustle and bustle. Going on a hike can increase your blood flow, stimulate your brain, help you relax, and allow you to connect with your heart. Even if your are not a great hiker. Even a mile-long walk, and walking through an arboretum's path can be just as rejuvenating as the Rocky Mountains.

Self-love of the body does not mean being physically active. Mirror work is another way that you can show your self-love towards the body.

I've heard people take out all their mirrors to improve their health. This does not have to be the case. Mirror work can be easy, but it can be challenging, especially if there are issues with your self-image. But, I encourage it. All you need to do to begin mirror work is simply look at the mirror. It may sound silly but it's something you need. You can modify it to say something completely new. Speaking confidence, love, self-worth, and importance to oneself is crucial. You can start by starting with one day per day. Next, try to do it every time you look at a mirror.

You must be honest with yourself and your mind to determine when self-love should be practiced for your body. Here is a list with questions that will help you decide how to love your body.

1. Are you feeling overwhelmed?

2. What does your body desire when you are all alone? Are you looking for silence, stillness, activity, or energy? Be aware that neither is better than either.

3. If you feel your body needs stillness, try lighting a few candles and taking a bath. Give your body permission to be.

4. Try going for a walk, asking a friend to grab a drink, or getting a group together to play card game.

Everyone has a different view of self-love. That's the beauty of the practice. With open arms, you can find peace and joy in whatever brings your happiness. The best practice is one that you can do for your body. It will change as you develop and grow. Keep your practice in check, but be flexible with your body.

Acceptance

Self-love refers to acceptance. Acceptance is the ability to accept your body, mind, & heart. Who you accept to be is determined by what you accept to live with. Accept the Universe's gift of magnetism and accept it. Only you can create that special magnetism. Embrace it.

The first step to making positive change in yourself is accepting that you have trouble with self-criticizing thinking. The Universe may be sending some tough things at the moment. It's okay to feel that full force and come to terms.

To accept your body can take years of effort, sometimes even a lifetime. The voices that you heard as a child from those around you could have been very negative or nonexistent. You have the power to change that. Learn to be kind to yourself. The curves and metabolism, as well as the color and texture of your body are yours. You can't take them away, and only you can have power over them. Many people have struggled to overcome eating disorders and body dysmorphia. Accepting your body is powerful and can make a huge difference in your life. Our bodies hold so much. Our memories, loves, passions and ideas are stored within our bodies.

However, I cannot tell you body positivity will be something that you can find within yourself every day. This is unrealistic. It is unrealistic to expect perfection if your body doesn't reflect positivity. This expectation is very high, and it can feel more like a burden than freedom. However, if you feel unhappy about your body right now, don't be afraid to accept it. You can return to a mindfulness of your body and accept the negative emotions. It is healthier for your mental, and even your heart health to accept the negative moments than to pretend they don't exist.

It is possible to accept your body and not allow negative voices to influence it. To put it another way, if friends or family members make passive comments about you and your outer appearance, stop allowing them to influence that part of your daily life. All of us have been the recipients of comments. They can sound like, "Oh you're getting another plate?" or "Are these pants your favorite?" This is something you should not allow to happen in your head and space. But it will not be easy to stop making passive aggressive comments about your body.

Body acceptance doesn't have to mean body positivity. You can accept your body's limits and honour them. Even though you were once a professional sportsman, you now realize that your body is not the same. Perhaps you won track meets as a high school athlete, but now you notice that your body reacts differently to speed. Be kind to yourself and listen to what your body is telling you. Your body grows as it needs. If you feel your body is getting worse after a workout, take a step back. Some soreness is okay, as it means our muscles are growing stronger. However, if you feel your body is not moving well or is hurting from trying to push past the same limits that you did at 17, perhaps it is time to consider a reevaluate. For many people, acceptance of the body means different things. Take some time to listen to your body, and then accept it for it.

Another concept that goes beyond body acceptance is body neutrality. This concept says that there is no good and bad thing about your body. Only what is. Our culture has a corrupt view of body positivity. The conversation is slowly changing to something healthier but still revolves around believing that everyone's body is beautiful, except our own. Another way to explain this is that when you see someone walking down a street, you think, "They are rocking their skin." Then, you take a look at yourself and consider how you compare your body to them, whether you were consciously or subconsciously doing so. To be body neutral, you look at yourself and say, "This Is what I have and it is something I need to respect and love."

To accept your body, you must first work within your heart and mind. It is just as important to accept your heart, mind and body.

I once knew a girl who had neurodiversity. She hated being herself. She felt unworthy, unloveable and unloveable for so many years. Every time we would have a chat, she would recount her childhood stories. She was ashamed of the things that life had given her as a teenager and young girl. As she grew older, people discovered her and began to accept all that she was. She had to work for years to accept the mind that was given to her, but she is now able to look back and laugh at how shallow her old thinking about herself. She was able to accept her mind and became an open-minded and happy person. It's possible that your story doesn't involve a Neurodiverse mind.

Repetition of truths to your self daily is a great way to get started if it helps you accept your mind. Maybe it's like my friend, who had people around telling her what truths they saw within her. Or it could be you, in the room, doing hard work and repeating to yourself that you deserve space. Any method that suits you best is helpful.

It could be helpful to bless others with the truths they see in them. I advocate first accepting and loving yourself before you try to share what your learned with the world. In certain cases, it may be useful to practice speaking truths publicly. Maybe you could start with the first barista you meet on your journey to work. Let them know that you hold space for them and that they are in the right place. Giving yourself a little bit of self-love can help you realize that you are as loved as anyone else.

Let go of control is something that may change your life. How many times do you go back over a conversation you had with a coworker and see all the possible responses? Maybe you got mad at Uber for driving too slow or going the wrong way. Many people struggle to deal with self-inflicted feelings that are related with situations they believe they could have done better. If you are having endless conversations about yourself, the best thing is to let it go. This might seem like a difficult concept to understand and you might think to yourself, "I have tried that before" and it is impossible to let go. If this is you, it might be worth your time to meditate and take some time to ask yourself questions.

If it seems difficult to let things go, or if you have memories that are not as good, ask yourself these questions. Then spend some time in meditation.

* Do I struggle to let go if I'm not happy with the outcome of bad situations or because I don't have the ability to forgive myself?

* Do my thoughts need to be free from guilt for actions I should have taken?

* Do I have difficulty accepting the fact that I'm not perfect because I have trouble with self-forgiveness?

* Am my perfection? * Is it okay if I'm not perfect?

Most people struggle with letting go of such situations because they don't realize they need to forgiving themselves. It comes down to pridefulness. The best thing is that you don't need to be weak in order to accept forgiveness. It does not make it acceptable to do what was done to you or someone else. It does however mean that you don't accept the consequences of your actions. Forgiveness can be defined as the ability to accept what happened and then let it go. There is no reason to self-inflict pain after you've made this decision. However, forgiving yourself can be an ongoing journey.

Let's return now to the idea that meditation is possible. This is a great method to gain a deeper and more meaningful understanding of your own inner self. It's worth asking yourself why you continue to hold on to such situations and how you can change. Understanding if you have the tendency to not accept forgiveness or feel unworthy of forgiveness can help you move forward. You can be more open and accepting of yourself in this way.

There are many things that will occur when you begin to forgive yourself.

* Accept responsibility. Accept the fact that you shouted at your cab driver. Accept the responsibility of your actions.

* Allow yourself and others to grieve what has happened. This doesn't necessarily mean sobbing on a floor.

Accept the responsibility of what you did, acknowledge it was there, and let go.

The act and practice of self-forgiveness, while powerful, can be very difficult. It might help you to learn the right way to apologize for someone else. You can make an apology to another person. Then, you can do it for yourself.

Here are some things to consider when you apologize to someone. As children, most people learned that it is okay to apologize for something done to you. The act was meaningless for us as young children and we just did it so that we could continue playing outside. So how do we apologize? It works like this:

I'm sorry I did (state action), it made me feel (state how that person expressed it made me feel; unloved/neglected, hurt). I'm sorry. Can you please forgive me. Do you have any suggestions for me to improve how I deal with this situation?

A proper apology heals and accepts responsibility for the wrong you did. The same can be done with yourself to show your forgiveness and offer an apology.

You might find it easier to let go of guilt and shame that you have for handling difficult situations.

Even though you might not have handled an issue poorly, having high standards for yourself can lead to feeling like you've done something wrong. It is worth taking some time to examine the situation. From where does it come from? How do you encourage these emotions? Are those around you supportive of you, or reimbursing your negative feelings?

Have you ever heard that the heart is only 18 inches from a brain? It takes time before things get from the head back to the heart. All the things we talked about take time and effort. Accepting that you may have a slower heart to accept new facts and habits than the brain is okay.

Even if self-care has been a part of your life for years, it may still seem difficult to believe that you deserve it. Know that it may take some time for your heart to fully comprehend that.

It is important to recognize that you can't accept everything as true to you if it isn't obvious. Compatibility for yourself is key to understanding the heart.

It's difficult to change the habits, decisions and paths that you choose. Accepting and loving your self is the hardest task. These are things you have learned as a child. Be patient with yourself and allow your heart to open up to acceptance.

While all of these things are easier to write than to implement, small, mindful actions each day towards acceptance of our mind, hearts, and bodies is a great start to the Law of Attraction. This law is about self-love.

Chapter 8: Unlock Your Ultimate Potential

Every speck in scientific research on the subject human potential suggests that all of us have more potential power or ability than we are currently using. Do you know what your true potential looks like? Are you reaching your potential? Many people don't realize how many accomplishments they can make in their lives. We get stuck in a daily routine that seems to be working for most people and don't want to think about the long-term. We either refuse to do so or we don't have time to examine our true potentials. Unlocking your greatest potential is essential.

Unrealizing your potential can be one of your biggest regrets. Realizing that there is more you could do is one of your most painful emotional experiences. It is vital that you take full advantage of every opportunity. Here are some ways you can realize your greatest potential.

1) Discover Your Full Potential

It doesn't matter if you were born with innate talents or if you came from a wealthy family. Understanding your full potential will take you far beyond where you are now. It's the turning point in every successful story. The story about the famous poor man getting his lucky tale, or the How I Changed the World With My Bare Hands Story, comes down to one key factor: People who succeed discover how they can tap into something within themselves and live the life of their dreams.

Each person has potential in their own hearts. The great thing about each person is that they have their own potential. The potential to be a better individual, to gain more respect and to be more successful, as well as to find happiness and reach any goals we set our minds to. It is a combination of our genes and our environment. Finding out what that is is the first step. It can be very frustrating to try to live your life knowing nothing about what you should achieve.

The world has become a hostile environment and all the forces that pull us towards it are pushing us to the side. Learning to steer clear of the negativity is like learning how walk on a minefield. This instinctive process is often assisted by a watching parent or teacher, who may have spotted something in us as a child and called it out. For others it can be difficult to identify. It is well-known that most negativity we receive comes from our unconscious mind. It can hinder your ability to achieve your true potential, so don't let others' negativity weigh you down.

Environment is also important. The best way to find out what you're good at is by trying new things. There may have been limited opportunities in your locality or the lack of funds to travel. You might not have experienced the things that you are naturally skilled at. Your current alignment with all things is the best way to live more intelligently.

Take a second to consider the following:

* What are my gifts or talents?

* What is my strength?

* Where can you use your strengths?

* Where do I exercise my values and beliefs?

* How can we make a positive difference?

What makes my life comfortable?

What is something you can do even if you aren't getting paid? Our lives would be more fulfilling and happier if we all focused on what we are passionate about. Being passionate about what you do can give you the courage to deal with personal setbacks, to confront your weaknesses and to overcome adversity. It's easier to find your passions, values and strengths so that you can reach your full potential. Your passions are key to unlocking your potential. You will find your passions will naturally flow from your values, strengths, and most importantly your potential. When you feel connected to your passions it makes it possible for you to act every single day from your heart.

2) Unlock Your Mindpower

While you may not realize it at first, your mind can be very powerful. It has infinite potential. Once you have mastered the power of the mind and learned the laws that govern the universe, your subconscious can be reprogrammed to help you achieve all you want and live your best life. Each person on this earth has the same potential in their brains, but not all of them use it. It is the programming that we have from birth to present that makes us who we really are and what our actions are.

Your conscious mind is the projector of the current physical reality you perceive through your 5 senses. The subconscious mind works like a magic genie. If you feed it any information, it will act as your wish fulfillment agent. Regardless of whether you imagine it or not, the subconscious mind will accept what you are thinking as true and will work with you to help reach your goals.

Once our mind is free from fear, we can use it to conquer the fear of failure and to feel good enough. To let go from social phobias and hold on to limiting beliefs.

* Discover your talents and gifts, and discover how you can grow them.

* Learn how the identify opportunities to increase personal growth, and to learn new skills.

* Set goals that you thought were dreamers' goals and then accomplish them.

* Find a strong sense purpose and direction. You can make a huge difference by understanding the importance of your life.

* Be someone who loves to face challenges and then rise to the challenge. Discover the joy in conquering the mountains in your own lives and not accepting the status quo.

Discover the many benefits of a balanced lifestyle that balances your financial, emotional, and spiritual well-being. This will make you happy and content with your life.

* Stop living in the comfort zone. You will instead strive to live in an environment that is outrageous, fulfilled, and accomplished. When you put in the time to unlock your potential, you will be able to become everything that you were made to be.

You must identify your purpose. This requires you to look at your passions. Live a passion-filled life is one that's fully lived.

3) Find Your Passion

Passion is key to achieving your goals. Although intelligence, courage and connections can all be helpful, passion will always prevail. The true success of a person is almost always someone who is passionate.

Passionate about his or her work.

"Nothing great has been achieved in the universe without passion."

Georg Hegel, German Philosopher

Finding your passion is the first step to success in life. Once you have found it, harness it and make it your focus to achieve your dreams. You'll see the results of your passions and goals as you pursue them. Your life will start to fall into place. Being able to live a life that fulfills your potential is one the best things about living. People seek guidance. It's a contagious disease. The impact of finding your passions and purpose on others in your life will be immediate, without you even knowing it.

Now think about the people you spend the majority of your time with. What do these people do? Is their passion contagious? Are they an inspiration to you? Passionate about your work, no matter if you're building a firm or investing in real-estate, inspires others. It's a powerful attraction that can lead to good results.

Find what you are passionate about and then you can identify your main purpose. If you have lots of money, it is important to ask yourself why. Is it your main goal to create a collection of your belongings? Is it to provide food for your family members? Or to give you the freedom to do what you love? All these are different, even though they all require large sums of money. It doesn't matter if your purpose seems totally unrelated to making a living. Finding purpose doesn't mean you have to find wealth. Not everyone is wired for money. You may have a different purpose than your family, or your friends. It is all about what your purpose is and what it will lead you to. Give yourself permission to imagine your dreams and reach your goals.

Are the dreams that you have better or worse? No. It is up to each one of us to live out the purpose within ourselves. Imagine how different the universe would be if everyone did it. What an exciting and satisfying way to live.

4) Discover your ultimate purpose

Different people will have different paths that help them find their passion and purpose. If you have struggled finding the right direction for your life, or you just don't know what to do next, these ideas may help. Every person has a purpose. Each one of us is capable. To discover the truth, it's only a matter if you explore and investigate a little.

What terrifies or agitates you?

It's an interesting concept. But, what you don't want or fear could be the very thing that leads to your destiny. It's akin to the concept that yin is yang, there are two sides.

Fear could result from a blocked passion that you didn't know existed. Write down your fears and negative feelings. You can then look at this list and find an opposite charge to your fear. You may find yourself able to communicate your thoughts through writing if you are afraid of public speaking but love sharing your ideas. Is it fear of failure that you are afraid to fail? These things are crucial to our success and self-image. You'll avoid doing something if it scares you. It is often the most rewarding things that we are afraid to fail at, but they are also the hardest. Take a look at all the times you've said no or avoided something simply because you were afraid you wouldn't be good enough.

Who energizes you?

Don't let people down or make you feel pathetic. Respect others and work beneath them. That is how you learn the most. If you are not able to find someone like that, then read books on people you admire and take them as your proxy.

(iii.) When will You Get There?

Each journey begins with one small step after the next. You don't need to get to the end, but you do need to break it down into manageable segments.

You may find a little passion in something small and simple, then it blossoms into something bigger. Trust that process. Write down more baby steps to take today, tomorrow, and every day thereafter. Take note of your feelings as you go through each step. Notice how your world is changing. Find people who will be willing to help you along your journey. Yes, they exist.

Just as babies take their first steps, we all need assistance and sometimes fall. Just like a baby learning to walk, don't give up until you can complete the step. We've all been there. The most important thing to do is take the first step. You may find it frustrating to wait for things to happen if you are naturally a visionary. It's okay to wander from the intended destination. Sometimes diversions can lead people to exciting new places and experiences. Sometimes plans change. Be flexible. Be open to trying new things. It is easier to get there faster if you can temper your impatience. Keep believing that the universe will reward you for all your efforts. Faith and belief are key to activating the universe signal so it can know what you really want...

(iii). Are You Now?

Before you can begin to move forward, you have to be happy with who and what you are. The person that you are today is not the person you were five to ten years ago.

We all have a past. Our present is ours. Acceptance of our imperfections and limitations is necessary to move on. Accept yourself now. Love yourself. No matter the circumstance, any situation can help us find our purpose. No matter what the past has taught us, we can make a change in our lives right now. One person can be extremely effective by themselves. Do not underestimate your potential to succeed. Many people dream up goals that seem impossible, but they were not only accomplished but exceeded. Believe in your big visions.

(iii). Which Will You Do?

You can make a list with all the thoughts and dreams you have. It will be a guideline for what you want to do in life. Once everything is on paper, put together a plan. Sometimes consolidating, or regrouping, is the first thing to do.

Spend time learning or prepping. This is a great way to share your time with others who are working towards the same goals, to learn alongside.

Be patient even when times get tough. Remember that difficult times are periods for growth. They are where you learn the next important lessons. Chinese proverb states, "When things turn out well, business grows."

If you see every situation as an opportunity for growth, nothing is wasted.

5) Commit To Your Ultimate Purpose

Once you know what your purpose is write it down. Try to keep it as simple as possible and as clear as you can. A three-pager may indicate that you are still looking for your purpose.

Then break your purpose down. Take, for example: you believe your purpose is to host a talkshow.

The steps needed to get there are important. What qualifications would it take?

Is it necessary to change your appearance?

How would you raise your profile so people are aware of who you really are and believe that they can trust you to do what you do?

These goals can be written on a piece.

To stay on track, you can read these goals aloud at night and every morning. This is your journey. You don't have the obligation to share it.

Over the years, successful people across all walks of life have relied on their ability to control your thoughts and harness your mind. It's the common thread that all successful people share, no matter if they are business owners, or professional athletes. Find out how to drive.

Beyond our own belief in limiting belief, we have shown that it is possible to keep the mind on track and everything else will follow.

Transform your life by discovering the purpose that you were meant to live. Then, change the way that you see yourself living that life. Keep in mind that where you are now, is where you were when you thought about it.

Take control of your future and your subconscious mind. Then, you can learn to think more positively and take steps to make it happen. It won't take long for you to begin to reap the rewards from your efforts.

Chapter 9: Let Go Of Your Thoughts

The waves are created when you think, listen, speak or cry out. Meditation makes everything stop. Your brain can be totally still and unmoving. It's possible. Once the brain's surface is still and quiet, we can start to see and feel underneath. Other than what we see from the surface, it would be difficult to believe there's more underneath our consciousness.

Meditation is an easy skill to master. It's also very portable and accessible from anywhere. But you need to keep practicing it to get better. You might also find it easy to make meditation a second-nature or habit. The higher one meditates, the greater the benefits.

Empty Mind Meditation is a form of meditation where the mind is gradually cleansed of all thoughts that can interfere with the practice of meditation. This technique is known by Buddhists as Anapanasati or Vipassana. In ancient times, spiritual masters used the Empty Mind technique to achieve enlightenment. To achieve this state, they have to commit to years or even lifetimes of dedicated practice.

Common misconceptions are that meditation is a way to connect to the universal will. Meditation involves letting go the "ego", or self. The mind can be a powerful tool that sometimes blocks us from attaining the inner peace we desire. Meditation on the Empty Mind helps them relax from their hectic lives.

A simple practice of emptying the head can help one get rid of the anxiety thoughts that can clutter his mind all day. You can relax your body and achieve relief for some of your ailing body parts by getting into a relaxed state. A regular practice of Empty Mind Meditation is beneficial for holistic development.

Regular practice of empty mind meditation can improve the following areas: The Physiological Aspect of our lives, the Social Aspect of how we relate with others, Intellectual Aspect of how we think, Emotional Aspect, and Spiritual Aspect.

The Stages Of Empty Mind Meditation

An empty mind means a mind that is not occupied with selfish thoughts. Meditation is meant to awaken the universal mind through letting go of any selfish thoughts. This is a simple task that many people find difficult. Humans are wired to keep what we have worked for and learned. This is exactly the opposite to letting go. This is how meditation teaches us to let go clingy and limiting thoughts. There are many methods or techniques to help you achieve and complete meditation.

The simplest step by step procedure is what the most skilled meditation practitioner uses. It's shown here.

1) Sit comfortably

Practitioners should first locate a comfortable place to meditate. Sitting is most commonly used for meditation. Buddha is usually shown in cross-legged posture in almost all figurines and pictures. You can also sit on a floor or a chair. There are many options, but the most important thing is to sit straight and comfortable so your back muscles won't be strain.

For back support and comfort, you can also use pillows. Many meditation practitioners have used traditional sitting positions such as the Burmese, Quarter Lotus or Half Lotus. These positions are great for long-lasting meditation. To avoid distractions during long meditation sessions, it is crucial to be in a quiet area.

2) Relax Your Body

The next step of meditation is closing your eyes. Next, relax your body by relaxing one part of the body, either stretching, tensing or curling it repeatedly until you feel relaxed. Once you're seated, move your hips forward. Next, push your stomach up while tightening all of your stomach muscles. Relax between each contraction to release tension. After your stomach is fully tense, curl your back so that your buttocks muscles are visible. Next, arch your shoulders as you push your chest forward, tensing every muscle in your upper back. After each exercise, relax your muscles. Reverse the exercise, pulling your shoulders back. Push your chest out. Tense your muscles.

This exercise is good for relieving tension and stress upper body. Keep going until you feel relaxed. Start by arching your neck forward. Place your chin against your chest. Then, slowly relax. Look up while moving your head. Next, open up your mouth and screw your face. As wide as possible, smile while you tighten your facial muscles. As you frown, tighten your facial muscles. This exercise will relieve our muscles from the tension and stress that builds up every day.

3) Breathing

The third step to meditation is to be conscious of your breathing. Breathe slowly and deeply. As you breathe, feel your abdomen expand and contract. While you inhale/exhale, watch your abdomen expand and contract. Inhale from your nose, then exhale from the mouth. Reduce your breathing rate and maintain a steady pace. This will allow you to almost stop breathing. This will help to relax the mind and get you into a meditative mindset.

Clearing Your Mind

Once you're comfortable with your breathing, start to notice what thoughts are going through the mind. These thoughts should not be interfered with; you can simply observe them. Try to focus your attention on the place where there is no thought. Then, expand the thoughtless gap. Let it continue until there is no longer any thought. Gautama Buddha used the traditional method of empty mind meditation to reach enlightenment. Another empty mind meditation process is to simply stop thinking and just do nothing. Thoughts can appear suddenly. If they do, you should ignore them. Simply think nothing. All you have to do is close your eyes.

Chapter 10: Millionaire Strategies To Use The Law Of Attraction In Order To Reach Your Goals

It is hard for people to believe that thinking deeply about your goals will help you achieve them. Oprah Winfrey was a success story. How can you be? If you are able to understand it and take advantage of it, your outlook could shift to create a positive change in your life. Here are some of the ways that you can use law of attraction to help you achieve your goals.

1. Have a Gratitude Journal

Now you may think the law of attraction doesn't work because you just have to concentrate on what it is you want. To a certain extent, this is because energy flows from what you want. The law of attraction emphasizes gratitude.

Gratitude helps to keep you positive in your daily life. It is about listing the good things that happen in your daily life. Keep a small notebook near your bedside. Write down one thing you are grateful every morning you wake up. It might be the simplest of things like coffee in the morning, or it could be more complex such as family health.

Nathaniel M Lambert (et al.) have done a series of studies that show gratitude science to be a promising science. Their research showed that gratitude produces positive energy, happiness, and greater satisfaction. Journal of Personality and Social Psychology by psychologists from the University of California and University of Miami proved how important gratitude is.

Three groups participated in this study. One wrote a few sentences describing what they were grateful that week. Group 2 wrote about how they felt during the week. While group 3 wrote about how they felt during the week (what were their gratefulnesses and what was frustrating them). After two months, they felt more positive about their lives and were more optimistic. Additionally, they exercised and decreased their hospital visits.

2. Set up a Visionboard

Vision boards are simple yet effective. Vision boards are also known dream boarding. They allow you to curate images and quotes that align with your vision. You can display them on a wall of a board or on a bulletin board. You can use photos of any object, such as a house or Michael Jordan's image. However, this visualization doesn't mean that you will become a basketballer. Instead, you can channel Michael's intelligence as well as grace. Remember, a vision board isn't enough to make you successful. You must actually take action.

Visualizing is more concrete that just thinking about your desires. Byrne said, "The law ot attract is creating your whole life experience. It is doing this through your thoughts." When you visualize, you send a strong frequency out to the universe. A vision board does work, there is no doubt.

TD Bank surveyed over 1100 people. 500 businessmen found that one fifth of them had used a visionboard for starting their businesses. And 75% of those surveyed had achieved the goals on their vision boards. A vision board will increase your commitment and help you keep going.

3. Make to-do list

A 2011 study revealed that to-do books can help you increase productivity and prioritize your tasks. It also helps reduce anxiety. It sounds easy but it can help you get to your goals. You can start by writing out long-term plans. Next, break them down to short-term ones. Instead of making "buying the dream house" a top priority, write down all the tasks necessary to get there. For example, saving money, doing market research, etc.

4. Focus on the positive and think positively

One of the most important lessons from this book is to be positive. This is what the law of attraction advocates can not stress enough. Your energy will dictate the results you receive. Be positive and avoid negativity.

Positive people can be optimistic. However, you will sometimes find yourself saying negative things such as "I don't want this assignment to go wrong." Instead, you can say, "I want my assignment completed successfully."

An exciting study by Stanford University in 2018 focused on positivity and its effects. The study involved 240 kids aged between 7 and 10 years. It was conducted with 240 children between 7 and 10 years of age. The results showed that children who were positive answered more math questions. This resulted in an increase in problem-solving ability and memory. So, get rid of "no"!

But how can you stay positive? Positive thinking doesn't mean saying positive things. You should also practice random acts kindness, manage expectations, be grateful, and count your blessings. Positive thoughts and words are not enough. You must have genuine positivity.

5. Use sensory visualization

One technique that Muhammed Ailian used to enhance his performance was sensory visualization. This method is perfect for those who struggle to imagine their ideal life. Sensory visualization is a technique for visualizing your dreams. It involves all of the senses.

To illustrate, if your goal is to lose weight, you can start to imagine how you would feel when you reach it. You can imagine how your relationship will change with food or how you will feel once you become healthier. The law of attraction can be channeled when all the senses are involved.

6. Multi-perspective Visualization

Add a third-party perspective to your manifestation. Consider a third-party viewpoint when defining your goals. The outsider's perspective can help you review your actions to support them or modify your action plan.

Brittanny McChristian and others did a study of 400 people to determine visual imagery characteristics. Results show that the first person can evoke more emotions and thus be more powerful. The third-party state is more useful in helping to make informed choices regarding problem-solving.

7. Manage self-limiting beliefs

A 2008 study in Journal of Experimental Social Psychology showed that people perceive themselves and others according to their initial impressions. It is hard to change one's opinions and beliefs, even if those assumptions are proved wrong. Our brains make our decisions based upon the thoughts and ideas we have over the years. Spend some time to evaluate your subconscious beliefs to see if they are hindering you from reaching your goals.

8. Practice affirmations

Affirmations, which are positive words you utter in order to overcome your subconscious minds' negative tendencies, can be replaced with empowering thoughts to help you achieve your goals. University of Pennsylvania's 2015 study found that affirmations could be helpful in creating neural connections to help break through limiting subconscious patterns. These are some of the affirmations you could use:

"I know what I deserve."

"I believe the Universe will give me everything I desire."

"I am working towards reaching my goals."

9. Focus Wheel Technique

The focus wheel technique is as simple as drawing a circle or writing on a board. After that, you can write your goal inside the circle and then write down positive thoughts. It allows you to shift your focus away form limiting beliefs and towards positive energy. For example, if you are aiming to lose weight, then you could write this:

"I will be exercising four days a weeks."

"I will make healthier food choices."

10. Include Others

It's true that the law od attraction mainly centers on an individual's thoughts and actions. However, it's helpful to have others around you who understand what you want. There are people that can help you realize your goals. If you're a blogger and want to publish on a platform for your work, it might be a good idea to get in touch with someone who has published an article on the same platform. Enjoy a cup of coffee with them and get to know their thoughts. Most likely, they'll be willing to share some tips.

Being able to share your goals and motivate others can help you achieve your goals. If you ran a marathon with your wife and signed up, it is more likely that you will be running every day. If you didn't know, you could back out.

How to Set Goals The Right Way Using Law of Attraction

First, you must know what your goals are. The majority of people who fail to reach their goals are those who don't have goals or fail regularly to review them. If you lack a clear vision, and don't know how to approach it, you could miss the opportunity to benefit from the law. Unfortunately, if your goals are not clearly defined, you will likely fail to realize them.

In order to be in alignment with your desires and the law of attraction, you need to set clear goals. You can set clear goals by following three key steps:

* Set your goal

* Keep it down

* Check in at regular intervals

You will be surprised at how many errors you make, even though these steps appear simple. Here are some steps that can be used to set goals to improve the use the law of attraction.

1. Know what you truly want

The first step to identifying your true desires is to set aside some time. If you ask the average person what they want, they will usually list it without reflecting. People will often tell you what they would like to see happen. It is essential to take some time to really think about what your deepest desires are.

This is your chance to reflect and take control of some of your most repressed desires. You can make a huge step by changing your career. But you might not be able to let go of the desire. Be open to the possibility of anxiety, your preconceptions, and let go. Ask yourself "If I could get anything in the entire world, what would this be?" Once you know the answer to this question, picture your life if the goal is reached and believe you can.

2. Your Goals can be made a reality

Once you have a clear picture of what you want it's time polish that goal. To make visualization easier, draw a picture of the end result. Find the most appropriate words to describe your vision. To make it easier to remember and affirm, write it down. To make it easier, use all your senses. Don't limit yourself to a photo. Be able to touch, smell, see, and feel what it feels like when you reach that goal.

unsplash.com

Spend at most 10 to fifteen minutes visualizing your goal. Some people prefer to make a vision board and pin images. Others prefer to collect photos and objects that can be used for reflection and put them into a box. Your decision is up to you.

The way you present your goals to others can be refined. Try to find as many words that convey your dream as possible. Keep them at a maximum of five to ten words.

Consider the best way to express your goal. Be specific, confident, realistic in your words.

Be sure to say it in the present. So, for example, "I have the love of my partner" is better than "I don't want someone who will hurt me".

3. Master the art and science of reviewing your goals

Know when and where to review your goals. Though affirmations and visualization should be performed more frequently, review of your plan shouldn't. A false sense of failure can result if your objectives are not regularly reviewed. It is not a great way to evaluate your weight, for example, if your goal to lose weight, you shouldn't be checking your weight three times a days.

The little things really do matter. Recall what you have achieved when reviewing your goals. You might brainstorm some tasks that could help you get closer. If you find yourself not moving forward, don't beat yourselves up. This is an opportunity for you to evaluate what could be stopping you from reaching your goals. Is it your negative thoughts, or lack thereof?

Use the law to remove roadblocks. Get positive thoughts, start keeping a gratitude log, and get to know your inner voice. It is possible to achieve success if you can set clear goals, visualize them and use effective self monitoring.

Three Types of Goals for Activating the Law of Attraction

Many people are familiarized with methods for setting goals such as SMART and RIGHT goals. The law of attraction is an example of a way to set goals in accordance with the universe. You must set goals that will activate the law. These are the types of goals that you should aim for:

1. Breakthrough goals

We call these breakthrough goals those goals that are too scary for you. These types dreams can bring us joy. The possibilities are endless when we see things that we have not seen before. These are your goals to activate the attraction principle.

The law doesn't magically make your apartment and your man come true. It would be great if you took responsibility for them. These kinds of goals could be a motivator to get things done.

Walt Disney stated, "Dare to Dream Big." These are the dreams that enable you to envision elevated emotions frequently. The positive state activates your brain and makes it look for ways you can achieve your goals.

2. Result Goals

These goals are quantifiable. For example, you could have a goal of losing 10 kg within a set time. Because they have a specific and deliberate purpose, result goals are consequential. Your subconscious will begin to plan how to achieve them. Furthermore, results goals can help you reach bigger goals. These milestones are essential for achieving breakthrough goals. A good example would be "I need to lose 5 kilograms by April 30, 2021." Notice how specific the goal is and that it has a date.

3. Progress Goals

These are short-term goals that you set, but they also reflect your long-term plans. They are vital in helping you stay on track. You can lose your way if you do not have progress goals. Review your progress goals regularly to make sure you are still on track for your breakthrough goal.

Tips for becoming a millionaire mindset for success

Mindset is essential for financial success. Most people are raised with negative ideas about money. People tend to think about the worst when they think about money. These thoughts can be frightening and uncomfortable, not to mention being plentiful. People believe money is evil. It is not true. Money by itself cannot be evil. Bad people are defined by how they behave.

The millionaire mindset, which is positive and optimistic about money, is essential if you are to become a millionaire. Here are some ways to create the millionaire mindset.

1. More Self-love

To become a millionaire, you must have self-confidence. You will never reach the level that creates wealth without self-conception. You have to achieve a healthy level of self-esteem. This is why it is so important to build a stronger relationship with your self.

* Take care of yourself

* You should set boundaries regarding how other people treat your feelings

* Pay attention to the talents and skills you have

* Learn how to forgive yourself for past errors

2. Be hyper-responsive

Millionaires take a proactive approach and are able to act in multiple ways. Millionaires can create businesses to help them solve problems like not being able to find what they want. They want to grow professionally and personally. If they're running a business their behavior is influenced by the current trends.

A person who is average would prefer to be proactive rather than reactive. They only make the changes that have an impact on them when they happen. Most people wait for a crisis to decide if they want to change. You can attract more abundance by being proactive and raising your vibrations.

3. Tune in and discover what you're great at

Although it may seem simpler to believe millionaires are perfect in all areas or have no weaknesses, the truth is that they are far from it. A millionaire mindset gives you the ability to sharpen your skills so that you can focus on what is most important.

Instead of trying harder to improve in all areas, recognize your strengths and learn from them. You will achieve the success you desire eventually. If you aren't sure about your strengths, you can think of the things people praise you for or those that excite you the most.

4. Change Your Views on Money and Wealth

Negative thoughts and beliefs about wealth and money can seriously hinder the law. Take down as many beliefs possible. Some examples are:

* "It is impossible to succeed within today's environment."

* "Success for people like us is not possible."

* "Rich People are Evil."

In addition to the beliefs, you should also make new statements. Example:

* "I can achieve success if and when I want it."

* "Success is available to everyone, even me."

* "Anyone may be good or not." The amount you spend doesn't make a difference.

Keep reciting your affirmations and stating the truths often. You will soon replace any beliefs that prevent you from realizing your dreams.

Chapter 11: The Happiness Factor

It is worth observing people to observe the happiness factor in action. Every person has the ability to be happy. But why is everyone so tight-lipped and unhappy? The reality is that their reactions to others can have a negative effect on their life. A child who hears from others that he is not worthy of love may end up developing an inferiority complex and feeling ashamed of his own self-worth. A girl with a more slender figure might be criticised by her peers and seen as less worthy than the rest. But, overweight people can still be happy.

Self-Esteem

If you look around a crowd or in a shopping center, you'll see that many people display happiness. While they come in many shapes and sizes, their uniqueness is the fact that they are happy with themselves. They may not want their hair to be curly or gray for fashion reasons, but they are content with who they are. They are independent. They don't rely on others to cover their weaknesses. And when you are attractive to people and love yourself enough to feel good, it will be easier to attract positive people.

You stop the law o' attraction from working if you allow self-esteem issues to get in your way. It's almost like carrying an advertising sign with big words on your back.

I am unacceptable.

I am incomplete.

I am ugly.

I am not worthy to be known as a friend.

This is all absurd. You don't have to be unacceptable because your mind says so. Your thoughts only tell you that you aren't complete. You are only as ugly as you make yourself out to be.

People with low self esteem won't attract people who are the right type. The underdog is the one who allows himself to be perceived as inferior to others. You can see that people will make unreasonable demands of you. But people with low selfesteem accept that they must serve other people and follow their lead. They don't. They let themselves be reduced to doormats by believing that they don't have any merit.

Observation exercise

Pay attention to people and look for the ones who are happy and stable. These are people who attract positive interactions, positive friendships and positive relationships. It is easy to love yourself and achieve this. But that doesn't mean to be selfish. It is important that you have self-respect and feel comfortable with who you really are. Do you really like yourself? How are you going to attract positive people?

You can look at the positive qualities of positive people and remind yourself to be more optimistic. Learn from their example. Be positive and you'll find people naturally drawn to you. If you like yourself, it is possible to start a conversation with other people. It is possible to work on your self-acceptance if you have difficulty with that. Make a positive mental note of every negative thing you think about yourself. Instead of dwelling on your problems, be happy for someone else and make them smile. It's up you to be positive, not to be needy. When you're happy and positive, the Law of Attraction opens up so many doors that your life can be full of joy and purpose.

You can't be happy if you dwell on the past. You can't dwell on your past. The past has passed. Worrying about tomorrow is no help. It isn't yet here. You can't change who you are if it isn't right now. All those unneeded worries are unnecessary. It may be that you have been victim to circumstances, but you don't stay one as long you view yourself as a victim. Once you are able to look within and not feel guilty about how you have been treated, you will see that the Law of Attraction draws people to your side. You're not a victim. You are not inherently negative. You're someone who can use positive drive and energy for a better world. Get rid of toxic friends. Find friends who make your life easier and the world becomes a better place.

Chapter 12: Myths Or Truths

It can sometimes be hard to discern the reality from fiction after so much has been written about the law. While most people accept the principles as they are, there are still many who doubt them. To help you recognize the truth and falsehood, I have included some suggestions in this paragraph.

I would need to write a book to discuss the myriad myths, legends, and lies that have been interwoven in this law. You will not be able to feel the effects of the law. It does not have to be a decorated home, with aluminum foil and gems under your bed, or with magnetic bracelets.

There can be no confusion or error in the law's meaning. Bad interpretation can however be frustrating and can lead to poor decisions.

What impact does our mental attitude make on our success?

One of the most common myths associated with the law o f attraction is the belief that we are attracted to false forces. Many believe that by having a positive attitude toward a problem or difficult circumstance, the situation will disappear. This is not true. This attitude, however can help to change the negative effects of the situation on the individual's lives.

Do you notice the difference? The most important thing is not what our current situation is, but how we react to it. If you've planned a trip out to the park with family for your birthday celebration, and it rains heavily that day, it is likely to ruin your day. A positive person knows that the rain will not stop but his attitude will. However, he will not allow an event over which he does not have control to spoil such a special occasion. The emotions and memories that are created by this day's unforeseen events will depend on the attitude the person adopts. It's not easy to overcome challenges or make the most out of unexpected circumstances. You can still hear their stories a year later about how the rain destroyed their previous birthday.

Many people find it easier to talk about a problem than actually solving it. They put a dark cloud on themselves and fail to realize that they can't truly be happy and strong without letting go of the setbacks.

Sometimes we feel angry or curse the day that a car has dripped our shoes. Instead, we should be grateful for the beauty and wonders of nature. Even a grey sky is beautiful. Every snowflake and raindrop holds a miracle. This is why we shouldn't ignore it and feel only a little bit of discomfort.

The power of an optimistic mindset is unimaginable. A simple ray is all that is needed to erase the shadow. A cheerful countenance is just like the positive and encouraging influence of sunlight which is vital for life and health. It brightens up others' hearts and gives them strength.

The happy face is a gift from rich and poor, young and old. Everyone has the right and can enjoy this gift. When we're happy, Al-les smiles back at us. It almost seems that all of Nature participates in our joy. All of the surrounding world takes on the same colour when we are sad, depressed and defeated.

When our smiles stop, our minds become full of negative images and are filled by doubts. When courage fails, disorder follows. Joy disappears and sadness is born.

The people who bring joy and optimism to our society are the ones that we need most. It doesn't cost anything to be happy in your own home. The contrary. You will benefit from it. If you leave with a sad smile, you're letting the world know you don't believe in yourself.

Positive attitude by itself is not enough

Another misconception many people have about positive attitudes is that they can achieve anything. People believe that positive thinking and concentration can lead to success. This is absurd. As hopeful as my thoughts may be, I am unable to perform heart surgery right now on someone who has sensitive heart conditions. A positive mental attitude towards the Olympic Games does not guarantee a win in the 100-meter race.

It is possible to have a positive mental attitude but not do it all. Realisticity is essential. This will open your eyes to the possibility that you can accomplish anything better than a negative outlook. Positive outlook will not make it easier to be the best, smartest or most powerful person, nor will it solve all problems. The positive mindset will allow you to realize your full potential, and help you achieve your goals. You'll be able to use skills more effectively. It will also help distract your attention from things you can influence.

We need to realize that attraction is only possible if we are willing pay the price. You might have to give up your old ways and adopt new ones or break off from people you love.

Though your thoughts might make the universe work harder to get you what you want; however, your actions must ensure that you get exactly the results you desire. You can't attain your goals through charity. You also won't get there if you don't take action.

I once heard someone tell you how to use attraction law to win the lotto. Many people think this is enough to solve all their problems. I've never been a lotto lover before. It's because I know we all reap what our efforts have produced. There is no shortcut or shorter way to this principle.

You might also win the lottery. But this doesn't mean your financial problems will go away. It has been proven that even though people are in financial trouble, many who win the lottery end up in worse financial positions or even go bankrupt. One million dollars cannot be managed overnight by someone who isn't able to manage 100 dollars.

How many times do I hear people saying:

"If I get raises, financial problems will end." Or, I can do liposuction to improve our relationship.

All of these ideas point to the desire for a miraculous cure, or a fast solution that requires little effort and doesn't require any change in behavior. It is clear that this quick solution can only be of short duration.

Do not search for the magic bullet. Examine the reasons for dissatisfaction and financial problems. Everything that happens in your world is simply the result of cause or effect. Every effect is due to the actions of certain causes in your life. Change the causes and the results will change.

The power of affirmations & autosuggestions

Another myth revolves around the power and efficacy of car suggestions. Use of autosuggestion phrases can lead to supernatural powers.

I believe in the power affirmations. Two-rock without positive affirmations may have some effect on our self esteem, achievement and success. It is important to recognize that it is not our intention, but our conviction that gives great power and meaning to the statements you use.

You can't solve an overweight problem by just repeating it: "I am thin, what am I doing?" It doesn't really matter how much concentration you have or how excited you shout it. If you eat with no control and don't move, then everything will remain the same. And your affirmations won't help. Maybe this is why people believe affirmations are meaningless. Instead, it's better for them to be realistic and just accept what they are.

So what is factual and what fiction? Repeated thinking is the best way to instill the original seed of an ideas into your subconscious. Repeating an idea enough to effect change in our lives would be like putting a plant in a pot. You don't need to feed it with light or water.

Confirmations made without taking any action are only intentions. As we all know well, good intentions can lead to no results if they are not followed through with action.

Can the law of attraction be used to attract wealth

Every material creation begins with an idea. But this does not mean that a thought is sufficient to create a new vehicle.

But if you don't have a clear idea of the car you desire, it won't enter your life. The following thoughts will help to create the circumstances necessary for you to make the car a permanent fixture in your life.

The question shouldn't be whether wealth can be attained, but how. Financial freedom is possible without relying on your environment. Al-les, all it takes to be financially free is to put your efforts into improving yourself. It is wrong that you impose your will on others, with the hope that they will do what it is you want.

If there isn't a desire to motivate others, it is impossible to get them to do anything. Each individual must be motivated. People often believe they are acting "for their own purposes", but the truth of the matter is that everyone makes the decisions to be happy, successful, and wealthy. You can't force anyone into achieving these goals. Most times, your efforts to force others to achieve these goals will only serve to distract you from your own purposes.

Make the best of your decision and use your will. This is the legal usage of will to obtain what you want for yourself, and to follow the right path. Make a plan with your mind and stick to it.

You will achieve success faster if your faith is more strong and steady. If you have the image of what you want, then all things will start to expand. You may have heard the phrase "The entire universe will swear in itself for you succeed."

This principle is easy enough to verify. It is easy to observe the results of negative thoughts. You will be amazed at how quickly doubt and lack will cause you to lose what you are seeking. Every minute you spend worrying or having doubts about the future, every moment you let your worries about yourself bring it, every month when you have no faith, that is another way for you to lose what you want.

It is vital that you are aware of what you think and observe. You must control what you think and what your eyes see. This is where your will comes in handy. It determines what items will get your attention, and which ones you will allow to take up residence in your mind.

Living a life of wealth is possible if you don't focus on poverty.

If you imagine the opposite of your wishes, it will be impossible for your desires to come true. The only way to get healthy is by focusing on illness or thinking about it. Also, no one can become wealthy simply because they have experienced misery.

Don't speak about poverty. Don't bother about it. Do not fret about the causes. It's your problem. Stop living in poverty and all the associated issues. You can achieve financial independence by investing your time. This is the best approach to fighting poverty.

Don't read books, magazines, or newspapers that are focused on the current poverty and misery. Do not be drawn to programs that paint images of poverty or suffering.

These things will show you that you cannot help the needy. It won't end poverty if it is constantly inundated in your brain.

Do not assume that by refusing to see images of poverty in your head, you will be able to spare the poor from their misery. You can't get rid of poverty by thinking more wealthy, but rather by encouraging poor people to have the thoughts and beliefs that they can provide for their needs.

They don't require sympathy. They require inspiration. Even if they are only given a piece to keep them alive, or a chance to have a conversation with someone to make them forget their situation for a bit, their compassion is limited to sending them some bread. Inspiration can bring them out from their misery. Help them to see that they can be successful. Show it by making your own money.

If you want to eliminate poverty from this planet, the only way is to make a large number people accept the principles I described of abundance. People must realize that the path to success is creation, productivity, not destruction of competition. He who eliminates competition will gain wealth. The one who is successful by opening doors to thousands of people can win. To keep yourself free from poverty, you must use your willpower to create a future that is bright and full of faith.

Can we attract wealth?

It's astonishing that so few people realize how your thoughts can impact your health. How we think about life and how we approach it can have an impact on our mental health and physical well-being. Strangely, the ones with the greatest fear of illness are the ones most likely to contract it.

However, there are many myths surrounding the law of attraction. Many people believed that the law of attraction could have supernatural powers. But the most important and real truth was often ignored. Is there any direct relationship between our thoughts and our physical health, which allows us each to take responsibility for our health. Where does reality meet fiction?

We know that brain function and the heart are among the most important organs in our bodies. Deterioration of brain functionality can cause death. The brain's many functions include maintaining and improving mental and physical health. The brain is responsible in distributing various substances that are important for our health. Endorphins act as natural analgesics. Gammaglobulins help strengthen the immune response. Interferons protect against infections and viruses.

There is increasing evidence that our expectations, thoughts, emotions and attitudes can influence the production of these chemicals. If someone with a chronic disease has a pessimistic attitude and doesn't expect his health to improve, it is possible his brain will not produce sufficient of the above-mentioned chemicals to fight the disease.

Many studies and medical cases show a connection between our thoughts with our mental and bodily health. Negative and destructive thoughts lead to many diseases and problems in the body like heart disease, hypertension and arthritis, skin disorders, digestive problems and migraines. Similar to the above, negative and angry thoughts increase the heartbeat and raise blood pressure. Anger, resentment or grief also weaken the immune system.

These negative attitudes and emotions trigger biochemical processes at the brain level, particularly the hypothalamus. Pituitary gland, adrenal glands and hypothalamus. This leads to suppression of or reduction of immune responses, making the onset possible of disease.

One example of this relationship between thoughts and emotions, and functioning of immune system is stress hormones. Cortisol has been proven to cause impairment in the function of immune cell functions. This led to the possibility that stress and other negative emotions like anxiety and depression might be the root cause of some diseases. Although it has yet to be proven that stress and other negative emotions cause disease, there are enough clinical data available to support this hypothesis. Studies have shown that positive thoughts like hope, rest, and begeisterung stimulate the brain's ability to release neurotransmitters that increase our immunity and boost our healing power. Multiple studies have shown optimism has a higher rate of chronic disease and infection than people who are pessimistic.

Chapter 13: How The Law Of Attraction Works

Because everything is energy, like-minded things are attracted one to another. This belief is shared in many ancient religious practices and spiritual traditions around the world. This belief, which is part of the traditional Chinese culture, holds that there is a vital energy force in all living things. It dates back thousands upon thousands of year. The belief in energy is also prevalent in ancient Indian spiritual practices.

This idea was not accepted in Western countries until scientists in 20th century proved it.

Quantum physics has shown that there isn't any solid matter in our universe. Your body is not made up solid parts. Although it's difficult to understand, this concept is not new. It has to do a lot with the fact all of life is made up atoms. As it turns, atoms can be viewed as physical, but not solid objects. They are composed primarily of three subatomic elements: proteins and electrons. Because electrons are so fast they can travel very far, they cannot live in any physical space.

A scientific study has confirmed that atoms are 99.99% pure space. They lack any physical structure. They are energy units. Everything is made up from atoms. Atoms are nothing but energy. You, your friends, your vehicle, and even your smartphone are nothing but collections of fluid energies.

Niels Bohr a Nobel-winning physicist said, "Everything you call real is composed of things that cannot possibly be regarded as real."

Beliefs are not facts

Why is it possible that two people have the same experience yet believe different things? It's simply because beliefs don't correspond to factual information. Beliefs simply refer to how you view a given situation. Your belief system is what you think about events, people, and the world.

These are psychological orders that can influence how your nervous and immune systems work. Your nervous systems is responsible for how you feel. This can impact your actions and affect your mood. Your environment, and your experiences, are created by your behaviors and actions. This is how your belief system creates your reality.

You have probably experienced at least one moment in your life where you were challenged about your beliefs. You discovered that what you believed was wrong. Your beliefs were proven wrong and you gained a new perspective. This could be the turning-point in your life. Our brain is a very powerful muscle. It can be hardwired to think a certain way. However, it is possible to learn, listen, then train our brain to think differently.

This is the first step toward changing the beliefs that hold you back from creating the reality you want. You can change what happens by changing how you think.

Identify what You Want

It is not uncommon for people to resist changing their mind. Because your beliefs systems are comfortable, you may not want to change them. You've lived your life believing one thing, so changing it can be daunting. Stepping outside of your comfort zone is hard work that many people are reluctant to do. When you feel content, why would you change anything?

What's the outcome if we think differently? Your reality has become your comfortable, self-limiting beliefs. Their energy frequency is unfortunately attracting a less satisfying situation for them. You are only making matters worse by believing that you will never make it big. You will always believe what you are told and not try to change your beliefs.

How is it possible for any other reality to exist? You have tried everything in your past to resolve financial difficulties. Because you expected financial disaster, you got it. This is the fulfillment of your belief. Your psychology congratulates this belief. Many people say "I told your so", a phrase they use often.

The problem is that this belief is just a belief and is not a fact.

Only you can believe what is true. It is possible to change your beliefs, which will affect your vibrational energy. You will attract abundance and wealth over scarcity and financial problems.

First, look at what is happening in your life. Then you can start to create a new reality. Your stubborn and limited beliefs about yourself won't let you change your mind. They are content just the way they are. Your brain and nervous sistem know you're alive.

It can be difficult for people to see the roots of their beliefs, so do something easier. Determine what it is that you truly desire. Instead of focusing on your beliefs, you can put them aside and identify the things that will help you create the life you desire. You can do this by asking yourself these questions.

* What is the most important thing you desire more than anything?

* What kinds of relationships would I like?

* What characteristics or traits would I like to possess in myself? What would I prefer to get rid of?

* What kind of financial reality would you like? How long would I be able to work? Would I ever work in a factory? What would I do? How much money will I need to realize my dream?

* What's my dream type of health?

* What goals do I want to achieve in every area of my life? It's important to divide your goals into short-term as well as long-term goals. Don't be afraid to dream big.

* What is the underlying motivation or reasons for these wants? What are the reasons I want to have what I want? These are the benefits of creating dream realities.

You might not care about changing your physical condition in any way. Your drive might be financial. It could be the exact opposite. These types of questions are important for every area of your daily life. The more motivation you have to change, the better. Make a list of all the reasons you have for change. A visual guide can help you see what you are looking for.

This is a great question to ask yourself about motivation. Do not tell yourself that your goal is to be rich. You need to ask yourself why you want a certain goal. You won't find any deeper motivation if you don't keep going.

Here's a sample.

Let's assume wealth is your first thought when you ask for what you are most passionate about. The next question to ask yourself is "Why do you want wealth?" One reason you might want wealth is because wealthy friends can travel all the time, which may make you jealous. What is the point of this? You respond that you have not been able to travel. People who can do so are inspiring because their stories inspire you.

Now it is time to get down to the WHY you want to be wealthy. This is an incredible motivator in your quest to get what you want.

It is important to make this as detailed as you can. To make people respect you, tell yourself that your goal is to earn $150,000 a year as a selfpublished author. Do you desire to lose weight This is not enough. For example, you might be aiming to lose 30 pounds and gain muscle in 90 days. It's the details, not the generals, that will get your goal accomplished faster and keep it focused.

Your answers should be written down so you can refer to them frequently to keep your energy going in the right directions. You should look at them every single day.

Here's how to identify and overcome your self-limiting beliefs

You can make up your mind about which beliefs you are healthy or unhealthy. For a long time, you have believed many of these self-limiting beliefs. It's difficult to change.

You can use a negative belief system to protect you from change. It is important that you examine your beliefs and set your priorities. If a belief hinders your progress towards achieving the goals you have set, it is important to admit that this belief is harmful.

You will discover that you are unaware of many negative beliefs you have cultivated. This is because these negative beliefs may be hidden from your conscious awareness. There are proven ways that you can uncover these hidden and limiting self beliefs.

You should look at the results of trying to overcome a difficult problem. Is there something that is keeping you back from solving the problem. Many times, it is an unhealthy belief or attitude that is keeping your from succeeding. You believed this thinking style was positive and could help you in some ways. You must recognize that this belief prevents you from attracting your dreams and goals. Sometimes, limiting self-beliefs can manifest as the following behaviors:

* You procrastinate more than you deal with a situation. You prefer to delay rather than take action. You can always do it tomorrow.

* Only if you are able to do it perfectly, you will be able do it. It is a belief that you must do everything perfectly if you want to succeed.

* You can tell yourself negative things happen all the time. These are just your circumstances, and they will always happen to you.

* Situations often force you to think about your fear. Fear makes you hesitate.

* Your negative self-talk. Your inner voice cannot see the positive in any situation and instead expresses them in negative terms.

* You worry over the "what if?" result of failure.

* You jump to negative conclusions despite not having enough evidence.

* To make an excuse, your knee-jerk reaction will be to apologize.

It is normal to complain about your current life, and how hard it is to start a new life.

Now look again at the items that you would like to have. What's the first thing you think of when you think about losing 25 lbs and getting ready in time for beach season. You think it's impossible because you don't have the time. This is nothing but an excuse. This is a lie. You have the power to attract extraordinary outcomes in your life.

Be strong and resist excuse-making and other self-limiting beliefs. As you think about your goals and visualize yourself starting on the path to them, write down any beliefs that might be stopping you from taking action. These beliefs are unhealthy, which can create negative energy frequencies and attract the opposite.

You can ask the following questions to change your negative self-beliefs and bring awareness to them. These questions can help you to focus on your important goals.

* What's the point of me thinking this is too difficult?

* What will I think to stop me?

* Am I making excuses for not taking action?

* What did I just hear from my self-talk? Did it use negative or positive language?

* What are my thoughts about the situation?

* What's holding me back from realizing my dream?

* I am feeling resistance. Is this where it is coming from? What is the root emotion that is causing this resistance

* Was my childhood fear of taking a stand rooted in something? If so, does it still hold true?

* What advice would I get from the dream version of me if he could talk to me?

* Is it really the most healthy behavior to have a knee-jerk reaction of complaining?

* Did I just believe that this goal was impossible because it is not something I've ever achieved?

Always remember that belief is an assumption. It's not true.

It is up to you to decide what you believe about a situation. You decide whether to hold positive or negative beliefs. We have provided a series of questions that can help you assess whether your current beliefs are appropriate to a situation.

If you are considering changing beliefs or values that have been part of your life for a long time, you may feel uncomfortable. You don't have to hold on to a belief for it to be helpful. If you want to alter your reality, you will have to modify your beliefs and actions.

Insanity is expecting different results while doing the same thing in the future. In order to successfully apply the law of attraction to manifest the life you desire, you have got to get rid of all self-limiting beliefs.

Chapter 14: Belief

What is belief, you ask?

Belief describes what we believe about ourselves and our reality. Belief can be built from the things we hear, see, or experience. It is how we perceive the world. Belief is energy.

The belief system is what processes our thoughts to turn them into reality. Each of us has a belief. Because belief is invisible, we have difficulty understanding it. Changes in our belief system are necessary to transform our lives, and allow the law for attraction to work. Understanding the principles and workings of this belief system is essential before you can alter it.

Every sensation we experience, every touch, every taste, every sound, and every word has an impact upon our beliefs. These senses can be found in the physical world. These senses exist in our physical world, which makes it easy to grasp their meaning. It makes believing easier.

If I said sugar is sweet and really delicious, you'd believe me. You would believe it because you have tried it. It is there, you've seen it. Imagine sugar as if it were not invented. As a new invention I might bring a bowl with sugar to you. I explained that I was working with this invention and created a substance. I gave the substance the name sugar. You were asked to taste it. It is really sweet. You would run probably a mile. You wouldn't believe it, it could have poison or taste sweet. You'd think it because you haven't had it in any of the senses or experiences.

Media has a profound effect on our belief systems. The majority of us watch television nowadays. We often see ads. Advertisements about aftershaves or new cars. Some are about fashion, while others are about handbags. These ads will contain hidden meanings. The hidden meanings won't be recognised by us. You will, however. Advertisements will feature models with full-face makeup and men sporting six packs. The setting will be luxurious, and the effect on the eyes will be amazing. The celebrities will advertise the handbags.

Why? Hint:

The answer and meaning are to make sure you believe this is what you want. Everyone wants to live an extravagant lifestyle. Everybody wants to look good. Advertisements tell you that you must have what they have to give. You don't know this. They could have put the advertisement in an ordinary setting, but they chose to advertise with overweight, unknown people. They chose visual communication to reach your mind. Advertising and media make up a multimillion-pound sector. You will not receive any return on all of that money. They know this because they are wealthy.

Your belief system can be affected by your surroundings and the people in your life. If you are from a poor or working-class background, you have a more likely belief system regarding money. It is not easy to find money. Money does not grow on trees. We work hard for our money, but we don't have the disposable income to live. To be prosperous, you need an education. You will never succeed in the real world if you don't listen to your teachers. You won't find many jobs, it's hard to find them. These are just some of the things we may have heard.

I was taught in school that writing and English were not my natural talents. My English teacher once told me that I would struggle to cope with the world. I will struggle to write letters and emails. I will need assistance in creating my curriculum vitae. My grammar is terrible. After all these many years, I still have all of my reports in a file under my mattress. I make mistakes. I don't know how to correctly format blogs, articles and ebooks.

I'm a believer and am writing an ebook. A blog is also my blog, with more than 100 blog posts. I will not allow anyone else to influence what I believe. My English teacher doesn't think about what impact he has on the lives of all those kids. He has not helped the education of the kids who came through his classes. Everything and everyone around you influences us.

How come so many people are successful? Meditation allows them to concentrate on their strengths instead of the physical world. Our beliefs are influenced largely by the physical world. There will also be a chapter on meditation.

The belief system is built in our minds, and we don't even know it. This is what constitutes the belief system. All these things are familiar to us for many years. Our belief system runs in automatic mode. Imagine a CD that is playing throughout the year. It contains all of the self-limiting, negative messages you have ever heard. You've been listening constantly to this cd. These beliefs are embedded into your subconscious mind. They aren't obvious to you, but they are. They are stored inside your memory. That memory can be referred to when you need to make an actualisation or decision. Then, you turn that memory into reality.

Imagine trying again to install a new belief system after all this time. You can't edit the cd with self-limiting belief. We need to delete the cd, and then start a brand new one. The new CD will be positive, with no limitations. This will be a habit that you will keep up with every day, every month, and each year. It is necessary to discard your old beliefs system and begin anew.

THOUGHTS

Thoughts don't exist and we don't seem to understand much about them. Invisible things make us doubt our belief in them. Maybe because it's not visible in the physical, we don't care. It's almost like our health. We abuse ourselves with junk and then see how it affects our bodies. Then we try to reverse this. We are all affected by our thoughts. It is essential that we understand our thoughts in order to change our lives.

To make a difference in our lives is to strive for a better life. We are not aware of the power we have as human beings. We are capable of becoming anyone and everything we want. We can transform our lives by changing our thoughts.

Every person has thoughts. Sometimes, it can be difficult to stay focused when facing a new challenge. This is something that we all have experienced in life. This is our thought as we go. The cold feet start to come to us through a voice in the head. The thought of something going wrong comes to our minds and we feel awful. This is called the thought processing of your abilities as an individual.

The majority of people believe our thoughts come directly from our brains. They believe our thoughts come out of the body. The brain does more than process the thought. To make the thought work for us, the brain takes them in. This is done so that we can comprehend and convert outside thoughts into physical reality.

A thought occurs to us and then it goes into the brain for processing. The result is a decision that affects our ability to continue with this thought/idea.

Let me illustrate.

You are driving your van or working at your desk. From nowhere, you suddenly have a sudden thought. Why not start a new collection of dog blankets, dogs coats, and dog brushes? Then you get a brilliant idea. It would be awesome and I could make some money.

The thought from the outside then travels to an individual's processing centre or command center. It adapts this thought to your individual belief system and abilities. You may hear the voice from your dog accessories. What was I thinking? There are already too many of these. The voice you hear may sound familiar. However, I am not an expert in this area. I will be ridiculed by everyone. I think it is best to leave it. Although it might seem like a good idea to someone else, it is not something I would do. This is the thought process of adapting the thought through your brain so that it matches your ability. But it is not matching your abilities. As you are capable of everything you want. It is your actions that can trigger this process to bring you better results. Your belief system is a key factor in your ability to achieve your goals. It seems like it will be a difficult climb. Trust me, this book can help you master this thought process if enough work is done.

I am an example of the other side. I sit down at my computer, and that thought hits me. It gets written down. I write dog accessories. I can hear it because there are so many others doing this. I try to replace or address it with a response. My response would have to be, I'm able to compete with anyone. I can do market research and locate the market's niche. I can research the cost of various manufacturers. I hear the voice and people will think it is crazy. I replace it with a response that will deal directly with the initial voice. I don't think anyone will think I'm crazy. I will give everything I have to it. People will have different ideas if it works. If it fails, then I have learned another way. I try again.

Learning from your failures and moving forward is key to success. What I am doing is challenging the thought processes and getting out of my head. This takes time because the thought process has been used the exact same way since the beginning. It's all about changing the thought process.

I will tell you where your thoughts come and how they help you. We must be able to see the truth and build the fundamental foundations. We can then use the knowledge and foundation gained in this process to continue building on it.

Our goals, desires, and plans are all electrochemical. These forms take place within the brain. The great thing about thoughts is not that they originate in the brain. Thoughts flow from outside our bodies. They come from the outside.

We live in the tangible, where we feel and hear the physical. However, there is an inner self that exists beyond our bodies. This is the source of thoughts. Your brain reacts to your thoughts by filtering them. We are what we think we can do.

Did you realize that we only believe we are capable. This is why we meditate when we apply the law of attraction. Meditation helps us disconnect from the world around us and allows us to connect with our inner self. We can let go of the physical and connect with our inner Self. Later I will address mediation.

Our thoughts can go through three stages. The first stage refers to the potential. The second stage is understanding. The third is understanding. Realisation is the third step. We didn't realize how simple it was. The good news is that this chapter will provide all the information we need so that we can master this process and achieve our full potential.

Negative people with little confidence and no belief will get negative results. What was my thought? This thought might be the answer they were looking to. It may make them a lot. The result will depend on the makeup of the individual.

When we get a thought it is like a newly-born baby. They are pure and innocent and full with potential and growth. That's how I describe a thought which comes from the outside. It is our making-up as a person that corrupts the pure thought. The second stage, understanding is what corrupts thought.

We try to understand what that thought is and put it through filters. Filters include our energy, emotions, beliefs, confidence, and feeling. Low energy, low confidence or low feelings can filter our thoughts and cause a negative result. The key is to focus on pure thought and not filter it through negative filters. This is how you get better results. This improves the process.

It is possible to challenge or override our thoughts and change how we think. This is our default setting. This default setting has been set up for over a decade and will be very difficult to change. This requires daily, weekly, and annual practice.

Brain glitch is the trick to override this process. The pure thought comes from the outside. For example, I'm going to learn to swim. The outside world is ready to allow that thought to enter the filters. You hear the voice saying I can't swimmer, and you tell yourself brain glitch. Then you replace that voice with something positive. The next voice is that I will appear stupid for learning how to swim at this age. Brain glitch: I will meet new people. You hear it again. It won't allow me to swim. Brain glitch, I can swim. I am going learn to swim.

This is a simple example. But the same rule applies to all negative thoughts. This is what you're doing. You are saying "Brain Glitch", which stops the process and replaces it with positive input. This is the normal process. But wait, something's different. It turns the process around to produce a positive outcome and a positive filter. It's difficult to achieve this with all our negative thoughts. We must overcome our old systems and begin a new process. This forces the neural pathway into a completely new direction. You can make it more powerful by using the same pathway for all your thoughts. This path is strengthened and it's our new automatic process.

This doesn't end there. We have to shift our attitude and energy in order to take the next step. These are just a few steps to changing our thinking. Keep this in mind if your goal is to manage your life. Each chapter in this book was written for a purpose. You cannot change your life, if you don't change yourself.

It is possible to attract positivity by using affirmations and visualizing. It makes your life easier. Use positive visuals to inspire you and make others feel good. It all helps.

Our next step will be to modify our vibe, energy and aura. This all makes sense and is in the perfect time. This all fits together perfectly and gives you the power to control your life. You want others to see you as an example and to look up to you. You want to feel satisfied with your life. You want it to be easy to get up in the morning and to enjoy what you do. You want passion in every aspect of your life. This is the way and how to get there. It's possible. With this process, I have transformed myself from rock bottom to top. It's possible if you continue to put effort.

Chapter 15: Rethinking Your Mind

Meditation is the first method to attract the Law of Attraction. You can do this by visualizing what it is you desire. The human brain does not know the difference between what we believe and what we make up. If you meditate and believe in yourself that you are happy, fulfilled and ready for love, then your brain will send the right vibrations out to the universe in order to bring you the companion you long for. Meditation can be used as a tool to increase the Law of Attraction. If you are able to take the time to remove all distractions from your life, so that you can concentrate on positive energy as well as the goals you have set for yourself, you will be letting the universe know you are in total control of your thoughts and emotions.

This doesn't necessarily mean you need to abandon all your morning or evening activities and sit on a prayer cushion with your legs crossed. It means spending at most ten minutes in the morning with your cup or coffee, and setting your goals for the day. It is the ability to focus on the love and happiness you deserve at the beginning of a day and then confidently think about your plan.

This leads us to the Law of Attraction, which is positive affirmations in your daily life that will direct your thinking towards the path you desire. You can do this by speaking loudly the plan you wish for your life. This tool is based around the idea that changing your thoughts can lead to a better life. Your mental outlook about the world can change by how you think, subconsciously or explicitly. If you complain all day and keep a negative outlook on life, then you'll only ever be able to create negative frequencies in the universe. Negative feedback is what you get back from the universe if you send out negative frequency.

Imagine how a young child spends their day. It's easy for you to see that the majority of them are happy and laughing, oblivious of any negative influences. Because they are sending positive frequencies out into the universe, this is possible. Positive affirmations such the "I love unconditionally without fear of rejection" and "I'll be my whole self in my relationships" are positive ways to send positive vibrations into your universe.

Affirmations follow the same principle as the saying "To walk the walk, you must talk the talk"; your brain responds when you allow yourself to hear what you think out loud. When affirmations can help your brain see and believe the things you want, you can really harness the Law of Attraction.

Hypnosis will be our final tool. This is not about having someone make you do the chicken move every time someone whistles. I am talking about changing your thoughts in order to live the best life possible for yourself, and the world around. If there are ways to improve the situation, it's not worth wasting your time, energy and thoughts on a person or relationship that you don't like. Your thoughts need to align with your dreams and passions if you want the frequencies sent out into the universe that will propel you to total and utter bliss. Hypnosis provides the tools to make it happen. It allows you to cause your inner mind to accept any changes you wish.

Chapter 16: The Secret To Attraction Law

Many people are trying to use Law of Attraction to make the life they want. Many people get frustrated with their lack of progress over time because they are not following the right order of manifestation. Don't fall in the same trap. Remember that you have to be the first. For your goals to be fulfilled, first you must believe in yourself.

Resistance from the outside world is the main problem people have when trying the Law of Attraction. The world seems relentlessly against them, regardless of what they do. It seems the more they attempt to achieve their goals and desires the more the world resists them. They fall prey to the temptation of blaming the universe and others for all their woes. If you want the Law of Attraction working for your benefit, it is a dangerous mindset.

Mahatma Ghandi, the great Indian leader who liberated his country from British control, encouraged his followers to become the change they wanted in the world. These words have the same meaning today as they did in his time on earth. You have to be willing to do whatever is necessary to attain what you want.

Let me go over this in more detail. The Law of Attraction will bring you any and all you desire. Anything you can keep in mind, the Law of Attraction can make it happen if your follow these Universal Law rules.

If you want to realize your dreams, it is not worth trying to change others or the world. You have to make the change within yourself. At first, focus on what you want and believe that it is possible. Then you can attract them. This is a bad approach if the goal is to change the course of the world. When you visualize the current external influences, you can hold in your mind what you don't want. You are telling yourself that things don't work out the way you want them to. The Law of Attraction instantly kicks in, and you attract more of that. Instead of attracting people you don't want, the outside circumstances will continue to work against it.

When you accept the world as it is, and allow others to be what they are, you can start to embrace the moment. Then, you will find your true power to create. While you cannot make the world better or change others' lives, you can create a positive change within yourself. This is where the real power is. The world around you changes when you begin to change yourself. You will start to attract people and situations that reflect your beliefs, emotions, and thoughts.

It is important to keep a positive attitude and be grateful for what you already have. You can even be thankful for where you are at the moment in your life, no matter what it is. This is the launch pad for your better future. Start with what you have. You are right where you're at the moment. Take the time to be content with where your are at this moment and you'll soon get there.

Once you have identified the things in your life that you wish to achieve, start thinking about them often. It is possible to imagine yourself already having them. This is what it means to become at one point with your dream. Your future vision will become a reality once you can focus on your desired outcome and allow yourself to feel, think and feel it. This is the key to your future vision. You can see this in children. It is a natural state, not hard to achieve. Give yourself permission to do this. Have fun! Enjoy it!

Let the Universe deliver what it wants to you, and be open to change. It is important to take action. There's this phase. "Faith without works, is dead." It is important to be willing to take small steps towards your goal. No matter how small, or insignificant, you can take some steps towards your goal every day.

You'll quickly realize that the Universe will take you in every direction you want. Chances are that you will meet people who happen to be coincidentally. It doesn't matter how positive your internal vision is, as long you feel happy and comfortable taking the necessary actions.

Remember, you are the only one who can make your dreams come true.

Chapter 17: Establishing Regular Self-Hypnosis Procedures

It doesn't matter if we are aware of it, all people use self-hypnosis every day. Marketing and advertising, as well as the television and movies, are all factors that hypnotize each of us. Your subconscious mind is a giant sponge that absorbs everything around. Everything you have seen and done in your life gets absorbed.

Your subconscious mind influences your life. This means that you will attract the things you desire into your life. In other words, what you sow is what you reap.

Truth is, all hypnosis requires you to allow yourself to become hypnotized. No one is able to be hypnotized at will, no mater what you see in the movies. Self-hypnosis actually happens all the times and is very natural. It is the state that you experience just before you fall asleep.

Self-hypnosis has the potential to unlock your true potential. This will enable you to reach your highest potential and help you succeed. Hypnosis does NOT have to be difficult. Self-hypnosis has many benefits and can be used to make positive changes in your daily life.

Hypnosis works in very subtle manners, which allows you to attract new people and new situations into you life. This can help make positive changes.

Self-hypnosis can't be viewed as magic. It is a process that requires commitment. Most changes take between 21 and 30 days to implement. However, persistence and dedication can help you get there.

The Consciousness of the Unconscious and Conscious Mind

Hypnosis refers to a general state of mind where you drift in or out of on regular basis. A form of Hypnosis is if you have ever found yourself lost in thought or in the grips of a great book or movie.

You can actually experience different states of trance every time you miss an exit or get lost in thoughts. Anything that causes the mind to wander stimulates imagination and creates an suggestible state.

The subconscious mind functions as an autopilot, where it follows preprogrammed routes. It will go along the familiar route regardless of your intentions. It is unable to steer.

Because it is programmed over time, r follows any instructions it receives.

Hypnosis is, at its core, just a form or focused concentration.

The conscious mind, which can only retain a very small amount of information at any given time, is the tip.

The subconscious mind (or unconscious) is where most of the information is stored. It guides our lives. All those little thoughts you keep repeating day in and day out will control your life. Your thoughts can become things, so it is important to stay positive. Many of us dwell upon the things that frustrate or annoys us. If you constantly tell yourself you're unmotivated or unsuccessful, it will manifest in your daily life.

Hypnosis can be traced back hundreds of centuries, all the way back to Ancient Egypt. It has nothing whatsoever to do or with the occult.

The subconscious and the unconscious are two distinct things. The amazing and simple way that Hypnosis makes life easier is by using it. Hypnosis affects the thinking process and thinking patterns at a deep level. This allows you to easily and quickly make changes.

Your life is a self fulfilling prophecy. Anything you dwell on or think of becomes reality. Self-hypnosis provides a way to get into your subconscious mind. There, you can easily make positive changes. It's very simple. To make a difference in your own life, you only need to think new thoughts.

The conscious mind can be described as the gatekeeper. It dislikes change. It likes things to be constant. It's very difficult for the conscious mind to make changes because it's trying to modify thought patterns and processes that have been in existence for many years.

Your subconscious mind records, replays and stores all of your experiences. You may remember being told as a youngster that you were fat, ugly, and that your parents believed you. You may still have difficulties with confidence and weight management if you have had a difficult life.

Although Sigmund Frud did not create the idea of the conscious versus subconscious mind, he did make the idea more popular and better understood. Freud used the analogy of an iceberg to describe the mind. The conscious mind is only one part of the iceberg. The unconscious mind, also known as the one below conscious thoughts, contains a far greater amount of information. He believed that we are fully aware and conscious of what is occurring in our conscious thoughts, but most of us do not know how much information is stored in our unconscious minds.

The more positive feelings you have like joy, passion, love, peace, and love, the more peaceful and happy you will feel. The mind will believe what you tell it.

Negative emotions, such anxiety, bitterness and anger, as well as feelings of shame and distrust, can make you feel miserable and lead to you thinking that you have done the right thing.

It's possible for the brain to be trained to think in one or another way. Even if your childhood was filled with bitterness and anger, it doesn't mean that you have to remain that way. The subconscious mind is where you can start to change your thinking. Self-hypnosis is a good way to begin because it allows for positive thoughts and feelings that are imprinted on your brain and subconscious mind.

If you want to live a happy and healthy life, then all you have to do is create new programming. A tool like self-hypnosis will help you do that.

Problem is, most people are too involved in the drama and the suffering. Instead of focusing your attention on the good, you focus on the things that are going well. Happiness can be found by choosing happiness rather than sadness. You can be happy in this moment and happy with what you do. You have the option of making different choices if your choices don't suit you.

Your life's purpose and meaning is determined by your emotions and feelings. Without them, life would be boring. You wouldn't know joy if it wasn't for the pain. Happiness would not be possible without sadness and pain. As the yin/yang principle, you need both good and bad emotions and feelings to keep your perspective. However, you can choose instead to place more emphasis on the positive emotions and feel and just move on with the negativities.

Self-hypnosis helps you to transform your life.

Imagination

Albert Einstein believes that imagination is as important as knowledge. The subconscious mind doesn't distinguish between imagination and reality. So when you replay a scenario within your mind, it takes it as fact. Self-hypnosis, visualization and selfhypnosis are powerful tools you can use to transform your life. The ability to use imagination can help you transform your thoughts and feelings into mentally appealing images. The subconscious mind sees those mental images and makes them real. In the end, your mind then brings those mental pictures into your life.

Conclusion

The mind can think of a million things every day. Never forget that you have the power, and the privilege, to direct thoughts in any way you choose. This power must not be taken for granted. If you are able to make it possible in your mind, it can be made real in real life. How amazing is that?

The law od attraction is so beautiful it allows you to grow, learn, and become better. It is as simple as waiting for your blessings and being patient. You don't get what you plant until you harvest it. Your past mistakes or successes do not define your character. Imagine where you have come. You've likely survived difficult times, and accomplished feats that were seemingly impossible. Your ability doesn't just enable you to get by. Do not remain in darkness when you have the potential to see. Do it again.

Never lose sight of the power you possess. The ability not only to impact reality but also the lives of other people. Give back to others and transform their lives with your kindness and smile. It's the greatest feeling of fulfillment to live with purpose and be of service. Keep a positive attitude and spread love. You'll be amazed how much you can have to be grateful for. The truth is that life is too short. Don't waste it wondering about the future.

www.ingramcontent.com/pod-product-compliance
Lightning Source LLC
Chambersburg PA
CBHW050405120526
44590CB00015B/1833